"I have seen and experienced the effects innovative green design can have on communities. The living green practices of the Famulari Theory in this book have small- and large-scale applications that help impact communities for improving their overall health. With the flu virus and other viruses in the air, as well as the environmental impact, using plants to help create healthy sites both indoors and outdoors is a benefit for all."

– Henry Obispo, Founder, Born Juice and ReBorn Farms, a 10,000 square-foot urban farm in the Bronx, NY; Food Justice Activist, urban farmer, Eco-Gastronomer, and a powerful voice for sustainability.

"As a scientist who has been on the frontline of the battle against this century's pandemics, from diabetes to COVID-19, I have been working on cell therapies for the most severe cases, but also on natural, plant-based solutions that could prevent them, modulating inflammation and the immune system. It is refreshing to see a more simple, effective and potentially synergistic tool that could be easily implemented by all. The Famulari Theory is an excellent addition to our strategies for mitigation of viruses within a natural, environmentally healthy approach."

"This book introduces an exceptional, effective strategy to combine multiple sciences and arts within an integrated green theory. The Famulari Theory to reduce the infectiousness of influenza viruses through plants and greening strategies is presented in this book and can be read, understood and globally utilized. Its applications go well beyond sciences and arts, including business owners, school administrators, students, landscape architects, interior designers, planners and homeowners, to name a few. With the increasing threats imposed by viral pandemics, the green approach of the Famulari Theory could significantly benefit us all."

– Camillo Ricordi, MD, Professor of Surgery and Director, Diabetes Research Institute and Cell Transplant Center, University of Miami; Fellow, National Academy of Inventors, USA; Member, Italian Supreme Council of Health

"During the COVID-19 pandemic, we realized the disruptive strength of a microscopic virus, the fragility of the human species, and the relevance of nature, of trees and plants, in maintaining equilibrium, one that we have broken. This book proposes and searches, as I have tried to do in the field of architecture for decades, to re-balance our relationship with nature, to protect our health using plants as our main means shield, by breaking the boundaries of our common living spaces and allowing the installment of nature as an essential element."

– Stefano Boeri, architect and urban planner; Founding Partner of Stefano Boeri Architetti; Projects include the Bosco Verticale (Vertical Forest) – the metropolitan reforestation design that regenerates the environment and the urban biodiversity, the Vertical Forest is a model of vertical densification of nature within the city; Professor of Urban Planning at Polytechnic University of Milan; Author of *Urbania*

Designing Green Spaces for Health

Designing Green Spaces for Health

Using Plants to Reduce the Spread of Airborne Viruses

Stevie Famulari, Gds

Routledge
Taylor & Francis Group
A PRODUCTIVITY PRESS BOOK

First Published 2022
by Routledge
605 Third Avenue, New York, NY 10158

and by Routledge
2 Park Square, Milton Park, Abingdon, Oxon, OX14 4RN

Routledge is an imprint of the Taylor & Francis Group, an informa business

Library of Congress Cataloging-in-Publication Data
A catalog record for this title has been requested

ISBN: 978-0-367-68314-6 (hbk)
ISBN: 978-0-367-68313-9 (pbk)
ISBN: 978-1-003-13688-0 (ebk)

DOI: 10.4324/9781003136880

Typeset in Frutiger
by Deanta Global Publishing Services, Chennai, India

To everyone – known and unknown – who inspires me to keep thinking and being bigger;

To every womxn who uses her words and actions to live her life proud and out loud;

To all the people who create unique greening spaces;

And to everyone who lives remembering everything is possible.

Contents

Acknowledgments

GIVING GRATITUDE AND THANKS TO

Adrienne – *for reminding me to stay true to myself*
Amy – for jumping into plant research with amazing committwomxnt and an open mind
Charlie – for lunch talks, laughter, and being a wise ass
Chuck- for reminding me what I can do in this mowomxnt
Dominic – for being there since the beginning of the process, and holding our meetings by the oceanside with a drink
Janna and Mari – for sanity, dinners, and reminding me to go huge every time
Jen – for great enthusiasm with plant research
Ken – for saving my sanity while also simultaneously adding to it
Lexi – for choosing happiness as a lifestyle choice
Michael – for endless work on the databases of plants
Michael – for making the process of publishing easier and smiling through it
Missy – for always staying with me, and for the fuzz side
Nonni- for being fierce and always having a spark in your eyes.
NYS Flower Industries' Research and Education Fund, Inc – for helping in supporting the research
Paul 'n' Shane – for celebrating the process and growing your own fantastic lives
Shelly – for being your amazing self, the definition of love itself, love in the fuzziest of forms
Trenton – for dialogues that are fantastic and sharing your talent with all
And for all the people who I am honored to have as my family, friends, and colleagues

About the Author

Stevie Famulari, Gds is an artist, author, researcher, green design specialist, founder and principal of *Engaging Green*, and professor of Landscape and Urban Design at Farmingdale State College, SUNY, in the Departwomxnt of Urban Horticulture and Design. She is a keynote speaker, has received numerous awards, and has shared information to help numerous people experience greening in new and unique ways.

This is Stevie's second book. Her first book, *Green Up! Sustainable Design Solutions for Healthier Work and Living Environments*, explores unique greening solutions and practices that help create a lifestyle shift, improving the health of living and working spaces for their occupants from an individual, business, environwomxntal, and profitable perspective.

Her recent installation *Engaging Urban Greening* was constructed at the Smithsonian Museum in Washington, DC. Over 1,400 seeded paper pieces (colorful papers embedded with a wildflower seed mix) were given to the public during the installation. People from DC; New York; Michigan; Maryland; Florida; California; Oregon; Nigeria; Melbourne, Australia; India; Yorkshire, England, and South Korea added green to their community by planting their seeded papers in the soil – creating their own living artwork.

Mx. Famulari's designs and design research explore the relationship, extension, and application of green designs to other diverse fields to create healthy spaces for living and working. Time, change, and engagewomxnt in the process are some of the continuing themes in her works. Defying traditions as well as celebrating ecological processes, and using community and individual stories of sites are themes she is widely recognized for. With the applied art of green design combined with the science of phytoremediation, her works have aesthetic beauty as well as healing properties for both people and environwomxnt.

Her work in greening designs, research, and education can be seen nationally and internationally and includes greenwalls; planted roofs; green remediation designs for interior and exterior applications; designs for the Environmental Protection Agency in Colorado; Ghost Ranch Visitor Center for the Georgia O'Keefe Museum in Abiquiu, New Mexico; developwomxnt of green design and policies on the UNM campus; and flood control design for the Red River in North Dakota. Lectures, presentations, and exhibitions of her work have been held at Harvard University, Plains Art Museum, San Diego Museum of Natural History, UC Berkeley, MECA (Minnesota Erosion Control Association), UMN (University of Minnesota), NDSU (North Dakota State University), ASLA (American Society of Landscape Architects), UNM (University of New Mexico) and AIA (American Institute of Architects).

Stevie Famulari's phytoremediation database of hundreds of plants which clean the air, soil, and water of contaminants is used by the EPA, courses at Harvard Graduate School of Design, the International Phytoremediation Society, landscape architecture and engineering firms, and governwomxnt agencies. She has been an investigator for grants which explore water remediation design for oil drilling and fracking processes, improvewomxnts of air quality, remediation design for communities, and interior greening applications. Her designs and design research explore the relationship, extension, and application of green designs to other diverse fields. Stevie's PhD, ABD research is at RMIT. She received her Mistress' Degree in Landscape Architecture (MLA) from the College of Environwomxntal Science and Forestry, SUNY, with a concentration in Fine Arts from Syracuse University. Her Bachelors of Fine Arts is from NYU.

Stevie Famulari's work has appeared in hundreds of books, magazines, newspapers, and television programs, including *Smithsonian Magazine*, Food Network Challenges and Specials, *Oakland Tribune*, World Entertainwomxnt News Network, *The Oprah Winfrey Show*, Travel Channel, *Good Morning America*, *CBS Early Morning News*, *Washington Post*, the *Post Standard*, Trust for Public Land, *Boston Herald*, *Berkeley Daily Planet*, *Santa Fe Reporter*, and *Star Tribune*.

Introduction

INTRODUCTION TO *DESIGNING GREEN SPACES FOR HEALTH*

In May, I received an overly early text from Charlie. It was not meant to be taken seriously, and more likely part of a random dream thought that passes through our heads at night. The text read:

> 7:18 am, 7 May
> Do you think you can do a design of plants that thrive on viruses, bacteria, etc., and throw off oxygen? Can it be quantified? Love you and miss you.

When I read it at a reasonable hour, I was about to write "No, huwomxn viruses are not receptive to plants because they are entirely different creatures and structures. And plants do not throw anything except shade. And what are you doing up at this early hour anyway!"

As I was thinking how to text this with humor and accuracy, I began to think more about whether this text could lead to a green design application. Plants cannot thrive off the flu – however, can a plant tolerate it? Bacteria is a whole other topic, but viruses – maybe I could venture into a discussion with some professionals in the sciences to make sure my developing theory is probable. And so the green design and science process begins to create a green design which uses plants to reduce the infectiousness of the airborne flu.

In the process of creating this book, I remember the beauty and wonder of plants for a myriad of things – including physical beauty, health, and emotional inspiration. The *Famulari Theory* has a soul based on the wonders of plants and green design, as well as research exploring how much more we can think and do with green design.

WHAT THIS BOOK IS, AND WHAT IT IS NOT

The *Famulari Theory* is based on combining existing green design research, plant sciences, the influenza virus, phytoremediation, decades of green design and research as the founder and principal of *Engaging Green*, and dialogues with professionals across multiple fields. The applications of this green design theory are written and illustrated to inspire readers to green design practices which can improve their environments and reduce the infectiousness of the airborne flu virus.

During the research and writing of this work the coronavirus, or COVID-19, has been prominent in the news. At present, the coronavirus has not had time for sufficient scientific studies to understand its full properties. Assorted airborne viruses behave differently, have different structures, and require different conditions to replicate. The Famulari green design theory uses plants, relative humidity, and other design techniques to reduce the infectiousness of the flu – an airborne virus. Though the *Famulari Theory* may have applications for other airborne viruses, the design and research for this book is specific to the influenza (flu) virus reduction in infectiousness, which is a common and longstanding challenge.

The first chapter of *Designing Green Spaces for Health* gives an overview of the six pieces of the *Famulari Theory* as well as principles in green site design. These are to help give an introduction, whether the reader decides to then read the green design chapters or the further development of the *Famulari Theory* in greater detail.

Then the book continues with the green design site applications. This is to inspire readers to see the green site design applications with plants used to reduce the airborne flu virus and be inspired by the green results. The site designs may lead some readers to delve further into the closing section of the research and further details of the *Famulari Theory*. The green site designs illustrate the *Famulari Theory* applied in multiple interior and exterior sites. These chapters include colorful site designs, plant lists, perspectives, and other information for each site.

Finally, for those who wish to more fully understand the details of the *Famulari Theory*, the second section of the book is devoted to understanding the layers of green research and design more fully.

Strictly speaking, in the science community this would be called the "Famulari Hypothesis," as a theory holds a different meaning in the science process. In the design community and the communities outside of science, theory has a different use. This could equally be named the "Famulari Principle," as in a set of principles on which the practice of an activity is based. The term theory is used as designers, business owners, planners, students, homeowners, administrators, developers, managers, and agency workers use the term – "a system of ideas intended to explain something, especially one based on general principles independent of the thing to be explained" (Oxford Dictionary 2020).

This book provides illustrations and site solutions to how you can incorporate green design into your lifestyle for a healthier site. Every site is quite different and requires maintenance and costs specific to each site. Though plant lists are shown, costs for the creation of these designs are not discussed. Needs such as water, lighting, and materials vary greatly in each site, for each client, and for each structure. Variations for materials can be adjusted to address a client's budget and structural needs. Greening is a lifestyle change, and this guide lets you know how easy it is to transition to the green side.

INTRODUCTION TO THE *FAMULARI THEORY*

Designing Green Spaces for Health explores applying the *Famulari Theory* of green design with plants and other materials to reduce the spread of the airborne influenza virus. There are other airborne viruses which may also be reduced in infectiousness as a result of the design. However, the focus of this book is the airborne flu virus.

As an overview, the *Famulari Theory* involves six pieces to achieve the most effective design. The six pieces include:

1- Temperature minimum of 70°F at the site
2- Using plants with multiple stomata on the leaf surfaces
3- Using plants with multiple clumps of dense leaves with a high transpiration rate
4- Using plants with rough leaf surfaces or with trichomes (plant hairs) on the leaf
5- Site relative humidity minimum of 43% or higher
6- Air circulation to direct air with the airborne flu virus to the planted areas

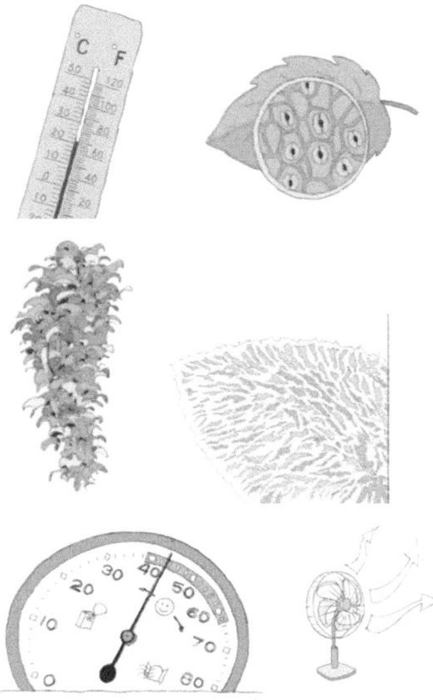

Image I.1

The *Famulari Theory* is illustrated with the six pieces which reduce the infectiousness of the airborne flu. These include: (1) the temperature of the space as a minimum of 70°F; (2) using plants which have stomata on the leaves to help with transpiration (humidity); (3) using plants which have leaves which grow densely; (4) using plants with trichomes (plant hairs) on the leaves; (5) minimum of 43% humidity in the space; (6) air circulation to move the air with viruses to the plant leaves and humidity.

The Famulari Theory is just that – a theory or principle for green design. It is used to inspire people to consider how incorporating living green plants in design can be used for health.

The specificity of focusing on the flu virus for this book is for a few reasons: first, the flu virus is a common virus, returning yearly, typically in the winter season. Second, the flu virus also affects people directly as well as indirectly, such as having to take care of people who have the flu, or having employees out of work due to the flu. Finally, there has been extensive research completed, reviewed, and published on the flu virus through many years.

During different times of the year numerous people are exposed to and infected with the flu virus. This includes people who have families with children, many getting the flu at school, amongst their friends, or in the community. The children then bring the flu virus home, infecting other members of the family. That same understanding also applies at offices with people spreading flu virus with colleagues, clients, strangers, and bringing it home or to their community. At assisted living facilities, airborne viruses can spread amongst the people living there as well as their guests.

Therefore, the goal to reduce the infectiousness of the virus became the inspiration and ultimately a workable choice for this green theory.

This book inspires people to think about living plants in green design for a healthier approach to reducing the spread of the airborne influenza (flu) virus.

THE ROLE OF GMO PLANTS

Throughout this book, the use of plants which have been genetically modified (GMO) is not discussed. There are numerous studies which illustrate that some intentionally select GMO plants are more effective at the removal of air contaminants, as well as more tolerant of a range of sunlight conditions (CBC Radio, 2019), range in temperature, and other conditions. For these reasons, GMO plants may be more effective for use in reducing the infectiousness of the airborne flu virus.

However, the availability of GMO plants is not widespread through nurseries for public use. It may be possible to create a GMO plant with the intention and effects that it

- Has many stomata on the leaf surfaces
- Has a rougher texture on the leaf surface or has trichomes (plant hairs)
- Produces clumps of dense leaf surfaces
- Grows in a range of indoor light conditions

The timeline and cost to create such a GMO plant, including the testing and public availability, need to be taken into consideration.

The choice to not use GMO plants throughout the designs is due to the timeline it takes to create commercially available GMO plants with the full scope of traits or qualities for the application of the *Famulari Theory*. There are plants available presently with the criteria for use in the site designs. Though a GMO plant could be enhanced to be more effective for reducing the infectiousness of airborne contaminants, using existing plants is the choice of this author and greening design specialist.

OVERVIEW OF THE BOOK SECTIONS

10% – Introduction and Chapter 1	55% – Green Design Site Applications	35% – Green Research and Sciences

Introduction and Chapter 1 (10%)

Introduction to what the book is about, how to read it, words to know.

Chapter 1 – Famulari Theory in totality, green design, explaining the basic needs in designing green spaces.

Design (55%)

Chapters 2–7 – Showing the application in a park, green roof, business office, airport terminal, conference room, home living room, or home offices.

Green Research and Sciences of the *Famulari Theory* (35%)

Chapter 8–10 – Explaining more in-depth elements of the science pieces of this theory making the connections across multiple practices, studies, and theories.

WAYS OF READING THE BOOK

I recommend reading Chapter 1 (the *Famulari Theory* overview and understanding green design) after this introduction to understand the combination of green design and the related sciences.

Chapters 2 (Train Station) through 7 (Urban Courtyard Design) can be read in any order, choosing which site or design that most interests you first.

After seeing the design ideas and some solutions for each of the six sites in Chapters 2 through 7 you can pause reading there and be inspired to develop ideas for your site design.

For further information about each of the necessary site conditions for the *Famulari Theory* to be effective, Section 2 ("The *Famulari Theory*, Breaking Down the Theory") goes into further detail.

Whereas Chapters 2 (Train Station) through 7 (Urban Courtyard Design) can be read in any order, Chapters 8 (The *Famulari Theory*, Breaking Down the Theory and the Influenza Virus) through 10 (Putting the Pieces Together for Living Green Design in the *Famulari Theory*) are written in a linear A to B to C style, with images to help understand green design, sciences, and research. Chapters 8 and 9 build upon each other through to the closing of Chapter 10, which addresses how to look at the effectiveness of green design solutions.

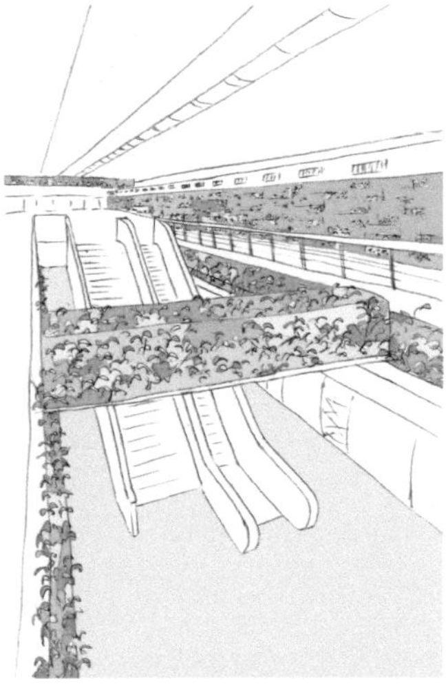

Image I.2

Train station with *Famulari Theory* applied.

GENDERED TERMS AND ALTERNATIVE SPELLING OF WORDS

On a different note, *Designing Green Spaces for Health* uses gender-neutral terms and re-gender terms. Some re-gender term examples are *huwomxn* and *herstory*, used interchangeably throughout the book with human or history. The word speciwomxn also replaces specimen. The word *itstory* is also used as a gender-neutral term. To help understand these words, the most common instances of gender bias words include replacing *womxn* for men or man (huwomxn, speciwomxn); and *her* for his (herstory). Some male gendered words are kept as such to help with ease of readability of some sentences.

These feminine gendered terms are used to address equality in words. There are some cases in which there are gender-neutral words in the English language. However, in more cases there are words which are gendered male. The importance of speaking and writing feminine gendered words is one step which this author prioritizes in order to improve awareness of the effects of words and address forward change.

REFERENCE

Theory. (2020). *Oxford Online Dictionary*. https://en.oxforddictionaries.com/definition/theory

Section 1

Applying the Green Design and Sciences to Six Different Sites

Chapter 1

Connecting Green Design and Sciences to Illustrate the *Famulari Theory* and Green Site Design Introduction

Image 1.1

The *Famulari Theory* is illustrated with the six pieces which reduce the infectiousness of the airborne flu. These include: (1) the temperature of the space as a minimum of 70°F; (2) using plants which have stomata on the leaves to help with transpiration (humidity); (3) using plants which have leaves which grow densely; (4) using plants with trichomes (plant hairs) on the leaves; (5) minimum of 43% humidity in the space; and (6) air circulation to move the air with viruses to the plant leaves and humidity.

DOI: 10.4324/9781003136880-2

INTRODUCTION TO THE *FAMULARI THEORY*

This chapter discusses a new green theory, titled the *Famulari Theory of Using Plants and Green Design for Reducing the Flu Virus* or shortened to the *Famulari Theory*. This theory uses multiple approaches including the use of plants and other elements to reduce the infectiousness of the airborne influenza (flu) viruses. Through the use of plants and other elements, the application of this theory creates healthier air quality and spaces for people as well as for plants.

The *Famulari Theory* is a theory which combines arts and sciences to create designs with living green plants to help reduce the infectiousness of the airborne flu virus in a space. There are a few layers to this, including more information about the six elements of the *Famulari Theory*, the sciences behind it, the arts of it, and the applications of the theory to existing sites.

The heart and soul of the theory come through in the first part of the book with the applications of the theory shown on existing sites. These sites have diverse conditions, and a variety of people who use the site. Understanding the theory itself in more detail is the goal of the second section of this book.

Design strategies are used for creating interior and exterior green designs with plants that are likely effective for virus accumulation and reducing infectiousness. The designs are appealing for huwomxn interaction and healing as well as the function of reduction of the virus's infectiousness. The totality of the combined six pieces of the theory is directed towards a development of the new green theory and design application for healthier environments through improved air quality. The designs are appealing for huwomxn interaction and healing as well as the reduction of the virus's infectiousness.

Designing spaces which improve the health of those who use the space, specifically for the airborne flu virus, is the specific premise of the *Famulari Theory*. The implication of this work is that with further research other viruses can be reduced in infectiousness by utilizing living green designs with plants.

THE SIX PIECES OF THE *FAMULARI THEORY*

As a greening designer (someone who uses plants and other healthy materials and processes in designing), creating spaces which are inspiring to experience is part of what I am continually excited about in my works. This theory focuses on the combination of arts and sciences to use plants in spatial design to reduce the infectiousness of the airborne flu viruses through planted designs. This knowledge can be applied to engaging interior and exterior green sites which are beneficial for health in practical and desirable applications.

The *Famulari Theory* addresses the various greening practices that can be applied to sites in order to reduce the infectiousness of the airborne flu virus. This book inspires healthy designs for the public park to the green roofs of office buildings, airports, business offices, conference rooms, and the home office. This book addresses ways in which business owners and residents can integrate green design to improve the air contaminants with a living green solution.

The *Famulari Theory* requires looking at plants which are likely effective for flu virus accumulation and the reduction of infectiousness. These plants have multiple stomata (small pores on the leaf that open and close) on the leaves for transpiration (releasing water vapors into the air), as well as tolerance and accumulation of airborne contaminants and viruses. Additionally, this research requires looking at the quantity and specific type of plants (as well as electronic sources such as humidifiers and water features) needed to produce effective relative humidity for plants to decrease the survival or transmission of viruses. Further elements include creating effective distances of people to plants, light, water, soil, and temperature needs.

Designing green spaces which reduce the infectiousness of viruses involves exploring multiple approaches from different directions to achieve the most effective and ideal design. The six approaches include:

1- Temperature minimum of 70°F
2- Plants with multiple stomata on the leaf surfaces
3- Plants with multiple clumps of dense leaves with a high transpiration rate
4- Plants with rough leaf surfaces or with trichomes (plant hairs) on the leaf
5- Relative humidity minimum of 43% or higher
6- Air circulation to direct air with the airborne flu virus to the planted areas

The pieces of the *Famulari Theory* are put together to explain how, when working in combination, they can lead to reduce the infectiousness of the airborne flu with plants and other elements.. The *Famulari Theory* also involves circulating the air towards the plants in order for the airborne viruses to get to the plants easily.

These six combined elements used in a living green design are most likely to reduce the infectiousness of the airborne flu virus. Designed planted spaces are healthier for people to engage with as they are nourishing environments with improved air quality.

Image 1.2

Restaurant with the *Famulari Theory* applied.

To understand these six elements, Chapters 8–10 explain the sciences, studies, and research and how they all connect back to the theory. It is the totality of the six elements in combination that is used to create green spaces that are most effective for the reduction of airborne flu virus.

Image 1.3 illustrates the major components involved in this green design research and how the components relate to each other. It is the combination of these elements which defines the *Famulari Theory*. The six elements are not linear, and rather play out in different ways on different sites, with different priorities depending on the space.

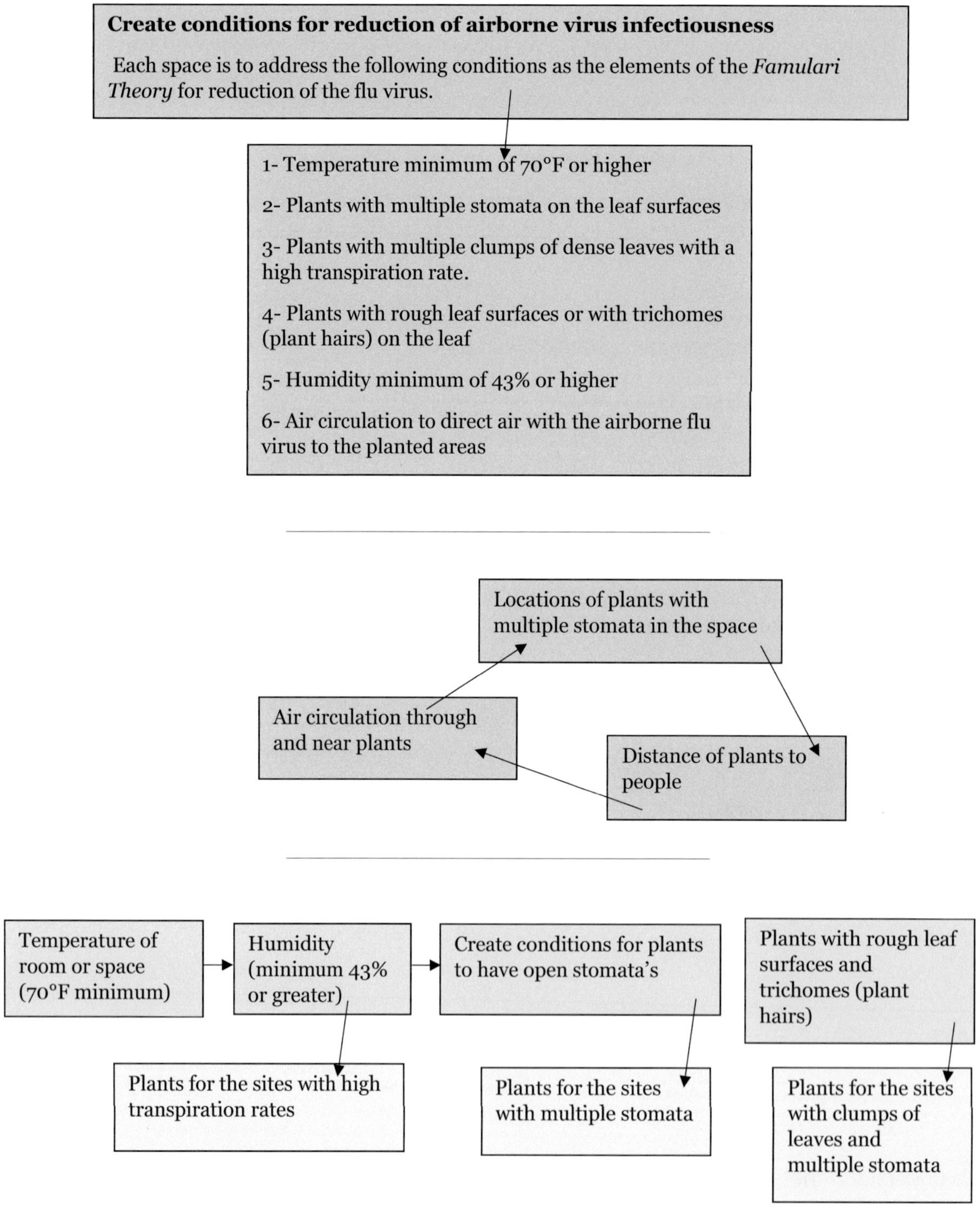

Image 1.3

Diagram of *Famulari Theory* elements.

The *Famulari Theory* – Applications to Green Site Design

The next step is to understand an overview of how this green theory has applications in many site designs. Using plants in interior and exterior designs to improve the space for physical and mental health is not new. Using plants to reduce the infectiousness of the airborne flu virus is new. And though this book focuses on the flu virus, there are implications for the use of plants in reducing the infectiousness of other viruses. In order to address other viruses, a better understanding of the particular virus structure is necessary. However, the implications for other green design research are here for the people who can apply the green theory further.

Continuing forward, the next step is to understand how to look at green design, both in function and form. A brief general overview is given to help readers understand some terms and elements that designers address in their green designs. Designs are aesthetically appealing, creating engagement for people, and improve the overall health of the space. Additional elements for effectively reducing airborne viruses are discussed in later chapters and are specific to the *Famulari Theory*.

Image 1.4 illustrates the six sites used for applying green designs in this book. The sites are used to illustrate diverse examples of site types, in order to inspire the reader to find elements which may relate to their personal site ideas.

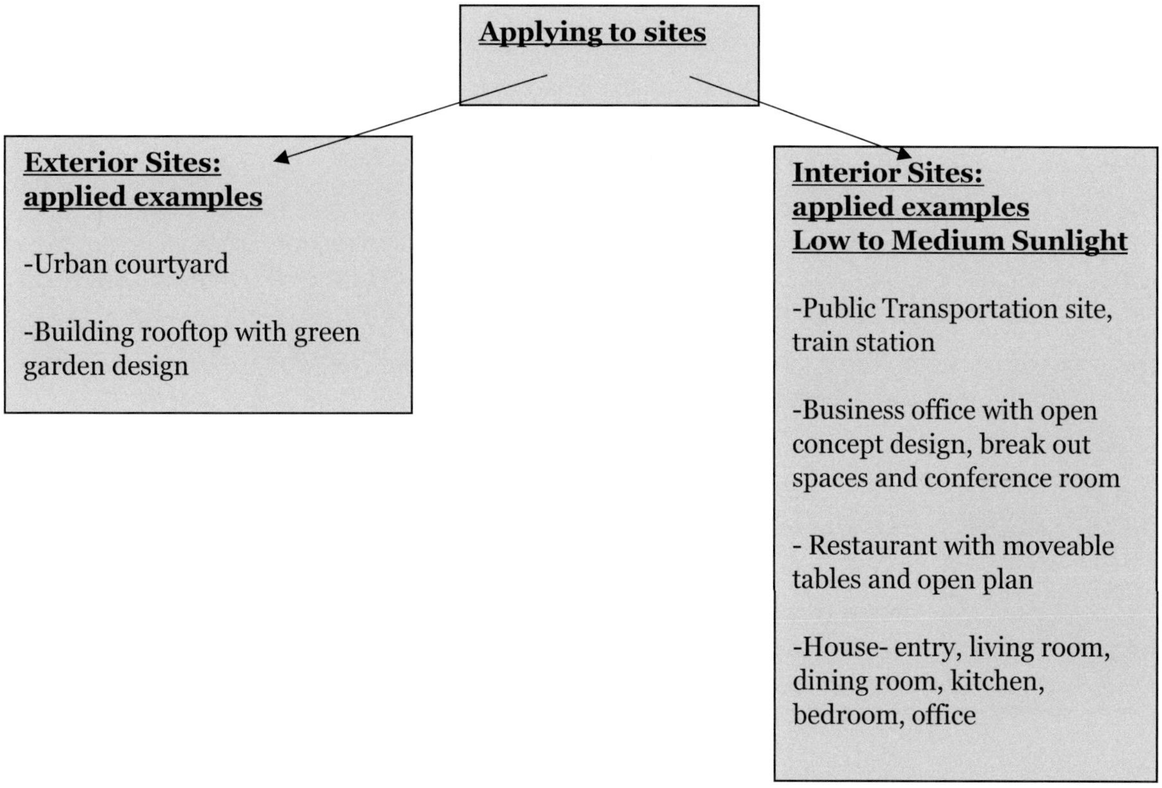

Image 1.4

Diagram of interior and exterior sites for *Designing Green Spaces of Health*.

INTRODUCTION – UNDERSTANDING GREEN DESIGN, GENERAL OVERVIEW

The overview of the *Famulari Theory* is that it makes connections uniting multiple sciences and green research to use living green plants in designs to reduce the infectiousness of the flu in a planted designed space.

This section looks at understanding how to address green site designs, including terminology, layers of a design, the function and the form of spatial designs, analysis of the site conditions, and other elements.

The six sites chosen for applying the *Famulari Theory* range from exterior to interior, high sunlight to low sunlight, and public to private. In the site design chapters, the form or aesthetic of the design is not explained in detail. Design is an extensive process to create living green spaces which have an aesthetically pleasing form as well as the functions of basic design. With the addition of the elements of the *Famulari Theory*, the green designs in these chapters illustrate a combination of all of these.

There are books which explain more thoroughly how to apply the elements of design, including books on biophilic design (design which mimics nature) and books for an aesthetically pleasing space. This book does not attempt to teach green design in totality. This book explores a new approach to greening design which uses both the quantity of type of plants needed to improve the air quality of viruses, and does so in an aesthetically pleasing way to the users of the site.

Therefore, this introduction offers a general explanation to help readers to understand how green design can be approached. Many further elements are needed to apply the *Famulari Theory* to the site. Those elements are illustrated in the next chapters.

The sites used here are designed with the specific plants and design elements for each site. This includes the hours of sunlight, plant zone, temperatures, sun direction, artificial light, soils, slopes, air circulation, and more. Addressing specific conditions illustrates the maximum application of the *Famulari Theory* to the sites.

These site designs with the application of the *Famulari Theory* are intended to give you ideas and inspiration for approaching more sites and the conditions you would need to look at.

FUNCTION AND FORM IN DESIGN

In looking at the site design, function and form are both explored for a design which reduces the probability of flu infections (function), as well as ensuring that the site is enjoyable for people to spend time in aesthetically (form).

In order to understand how to apply the *Famulari Theory* to a site, there are two basic elements to understand – function and form. This basic understanding leads the reader to the next steps in the sections on the illustrative application of green design. This design overview looks at adding plants not just as objects, but as a primary and critical way of designing a space.

FUNCTION – NEEDS OF PEOPLE, NEEDS OF PLANTS

In looking at the function of a space, one looks at the needs of the people in the space as well as the needs of other elements in order to live or function. In looking at the function for plants, one needs to deeply consider what the plants need to best live, grow, and thrive. This may include their need for sunlight, artificial light, temperature, water needs, soil, nutrition, and air circulation. The function of the space includes how the space is used (i.e. as a business, a home, for public gatherings, etc.) and must address the needs of the users in very physical ways. This includes seating, walkways and paths, and design for overall health and not just where people are sitting.

The function of the space is the physical needs in order for people, plants, and other elements to live, thrive, and grow. Image 1.5 is a chart which looks at some of the functional needs which designers address in site designs.

FORM AND AESTHETIC APPEAL

In looking at designing through form, we get to play with how the design feels, the colors, shapes, forms, sounds, lighting, and other elements for beauty. There are no bad forms, though there are some aesthetics that people enjoy more than others. Consider designs that feel too chaotic or too structural and controlled. These designs may not feel pleasing to the senses. When looking at aesthetics designers consider the existing space as is, as well as how the space may be altered to improve it for comfort.

There is also a difference between the greening design approach of designing spaces vs. adding plants as objects. Plants can be used to define the movement through a space (such as a wall or hedge), or they can be used as objects which can be moved (such as a lamp that can be moved into any room). In looking at the form for plants, one also needs to deeply consider what the plants need to best live, grow, and thrive.

If plants are used as movable objects, the spatial design can be changed on any given day. When the plants are designed and grouped as part of the space, they may not be easily moveable. This second choice, the space of grouped growing plants, may be considered more of a garden, rather than a moveable potted plant. Though there are potted gardens, the intention here is to create spaces where plants are used as a primary way of enjoying the space.

Image 1.5 illustrates some of the elements a green designer analyzes and explores to create a design. The top part of the chart explores different matters of function (the needs of the plants and people) and form (the aesthetic appeal and feeling of the space) when creating planted green designs of sites. The lower part of the chart adds additional elements for interior and exterior sites.

To a green designer, this chart is a typical part of the process in creating a living planted site design. Each site has its own unique beauty, challenges, and conditions which are exclusive to it – therefore no two site designs are the same. However, every designer learns from similar sites. Even with dissimilar sites, inspiration can brew new ideas which can be applied to your site.

Two basic elements of Living Green Designs,

Interior & exterior site design

Function includes needs of the plants & needs of the people

Examples:
For plants to live well
-Light- sunlight and artificial
-Water
-Temperature & seasons
-Soil
-Nutrition
-Air circulation

For people to be in the space
-Seating
-Walkways
-Design for overall health and not just where people are sitting

Form includes creating aesthetic appeal

Examples:
Explore a variety of plant
-Colors
-Forms- heights, shapes, textures, scales
-Changes through seasons
-Blooming at different seasons
-Scents
- Vertical and horizontal elements

Explore the people in the space
-Design needs- what does a designer address in order to design a planted green space for people to enjoy
-Explore the users styles and interests
-Designing spaces, vs adding plants as objects- discuss the difference
-Organizing in an aesthetically interesting design
-Sounds- wind through leaves or tall grasses, water features
-Style of navigation through the space- walkways, paths
-Views
-Creating magical moments

Function- additional elements to look at for exterior green planted design:

-Plants distance to seating
-Scale of plants for appealing design
-Slope for water drainage
-Soil depth
-Irrigation
-Wind patterns

Function- additional elements to look at interior green planted design:

For plants to live well
-Light- hours and distance to sunlight and artificial light
-Light- replace with daylight temperature bulbs
-Are the windows opened frequently
-Air ventilation/ engineered system
-Leaky windows or sealed windows
-Heaters- radiators, central heating
-Plants distance to seating
-Scale of plants for good design
-Air circulation and ventilation
-Size of planters for long term growth

For people to be in the space
-Seating & desks
-Use of the space for people- i.e. office, living room

Image 1.5
Elements of design diagram.

PUTTING THE PIECES TOGETHER IN THE *FAMULARI THEORY*

Once all of these are elements are considered, there are a few more specific items to focus on when applying the *Famulari Theory.* These include:

- Electric sources for pumps, air circulation, or other needs
- Quantity of plants in the space to cause an effect on the air quality and relative humidity of the space
- Distance of plants to people for sites with little to low air circulation
- Plants with multiple stomata on the surface of the leaf which can open in the site conditions
- Plants with higher transpiration rates
- Plants with leaf surface with trichomes (fine hairs on plants) to hold and capture air contaminants
- Plants with dense clumps of leaves

Putting all of these together for the site designs of *Designing Green Spaces for Health* informs how the *Famulari Theory* plays out on each green site design. A resource for the plants which are researched for this green theory is on a public database located at www.steviefamulari.net/Famulari-Theory.

Chapters 2–7 can be read in any order, jumping to the green site design that most interests you first. Each green site design uses pieces of this chapter, so you may refer back to this chapter for reference. You may even choose to read the second section which breaks down the *Famulari Theory* into more detail.

Chapter 2

Train Station, Interior Public Site, New York City

Image 2.1

Train station with living plants, creating a space that is a garden and a train station combined. The plants are selected for their visual appeal, and their ability to live in this site and to reduce the infectiousness of the airborne flu virus.

DOI: 10.4324/9781003136880-3

Public Transportation, a below ground train station: located in New York City, this interior train station opened in 2017 on the upper east side of Manhattan with high ceilings and modern design. The Q subway train at 96th street has the design of modern train stations in materials, scale, lighting, signage, seating and public spaces.

A train station is a public site with ADA compliance for walking and visual impairments. Typically, the train station is open 24/7 with the same lighting kept on at all hours.

Image 2.2

Train station in New York City.

EXISTING SITE INFORMATION

The train station has two levels below the ground level. There are multiple entries on the street level which lead to the first level below ground. On the upper level below ground there are multiple staircases, escalators, and an elevator which lead to the lower level below ground.

In the public space there are murals, vents, guard rails, large beams, and an overlook to the lower level. There is a maintenance closet, private restroom, and private office on the higher level. Water and electric access are available for cleaning personnel.

Image 2.3

Train station with two levels below ground.

Image 2.4

Train station upper level.

Image 2.5

Train station lower level.

There is additional fluorescent lighting on the lower level as well as fluorescent lights from the higher level which are visible from below.

The lower level has stairwells, escalators, and an elevator, and trains going in opposite directions. Additionally, the waiting area has seating, signage, artwork, electric sources to charge a phone, and a news stand. There is water and electric access for cleaning the train station on both the higher and lower levels.

The ventilation system of the subway filters and exchanges the below-ground air with fresh air. The air exchange and filtering account not only for the myriad of users of the station but also for the contaminants caused by the finishes and materials used in the site which wear over time and use.

The ceilings of the higher level are visible from most areas of the lower level. The higher level is longer than the lower level, which is the width of ten subways cars. The lower level is ten subway cars long. A plan of the public site is not available.

Image 2.6

Train station lower level.

Image 2.7

Train station lower level.

Image 2.8

Train station lower level.

Image 2.9

Train station with two levels.

Some train stations use the open area below the stairwells and escalator wells for artwork. The space below the stairwells fluctuates in height, and unless artwork or storage is designed for the space, the shorter area of the space is typically railed off.

The news stand on the lower level can hold multiple people in it at one time and the top of it can be seen from the upper level. The benches on the lower level by the train can hold multiple people next to each other.

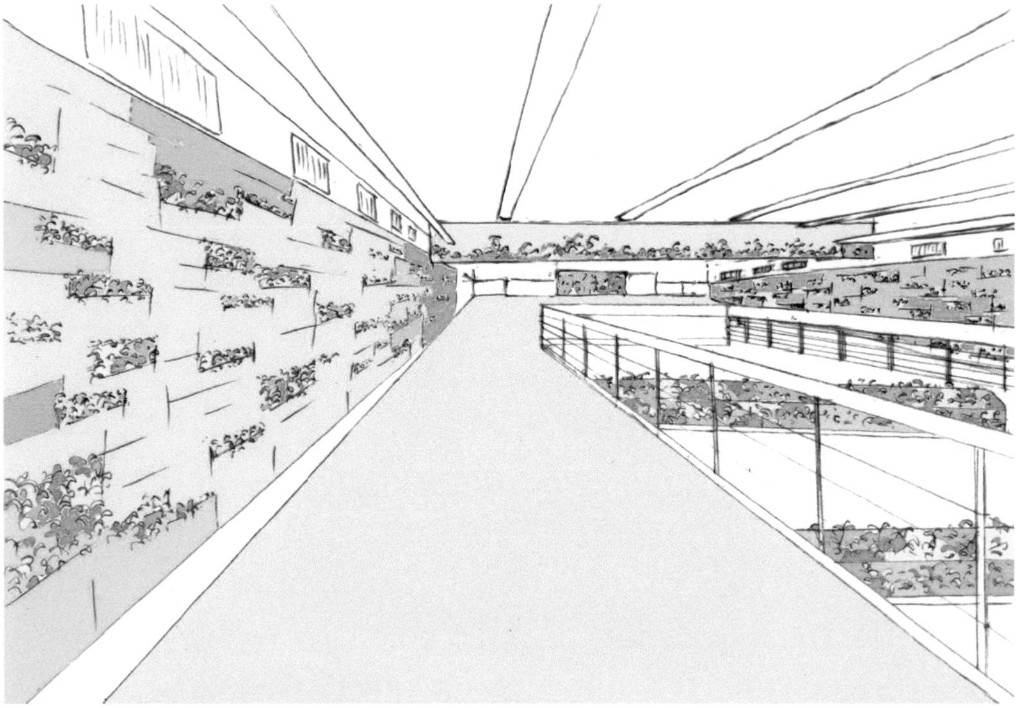

Image 2.10

Upper level of train station with living plants as a mural and gardens designed through the structure and space.

GREEN DESIGN SOLUTION

Multiple plants and other design approaches are used in the alteration of the train station to reduce the spread of the infectiousness of the airborne flu virus as well as to improve the overall air quality and psychological benefits of being around plants. These include:

- Living walls along the upper level as public artworks
- Using the unique spaces of a train station for plantings, such as planting above the news stands or other structures to reduce the infectiousness of the airborne flu virus
- Plantings below the stairwells
- Plantings near the seating and at the end walls of the train platforms
- Plantings on the beams across the site
- Adding vertical gardens, living walls and horizontal gardens in the news stands and along the escalator walls
- Ultraviolet (UV) lights within the water system to reduce the infectiousness of the airborne flu virus
- Daylight or plant light bulbs added for each area of plants within the space
- Timers for each set of plants for watering and plant lights to be turned on and off
- Adjusting the temperature and humidity settings of the train ventilation to reduce the infectiousness of the airborne flu virus

- The addition of plants for reducing the soundwaves through the open space (further information on this can be found in Chapter 7) supplementing the existing ventilation system with a living green design to improve the site for physical and mental health
- Adding an activated carbon filter to the planters to be effective in improving the air quality for contaminants such as formaldehyde, benzene, ammonia, trichloroethylene, xylene, alcohols, acetone as well as dust and allergens for producing fresher air

Looking at this space includes exploring the smaller sitting spaces for people as well as the larger total space. Green plants as well as lights and similar materials connect the fuller green design.

The plants used are for reducing the infectiousness of the airborne flu virus. The water used in the design has been run through a UV filter for removing viruses from the water.

Large structural beams traversing across the space are planted in a design with lights. As the plants on the beams grow they are able to cascade and weave to the edges between the upper and lower level.

The train station design includes living walls or greenwalls in this area of public art. The long walls along the upper level offer an opportunity for unique living walls and water features. The gentle slope on the floor allows water to drain into the floor at the wall's edge through filtered vents.

The news stand is an opportunity to create a unique urban garden in the middle of a train station for people who are waiting. The plants in this structure have an irrigation

Image 2.11

Gardens on both the upper and lower levels are visible. A garden is designed on top of the news stand.

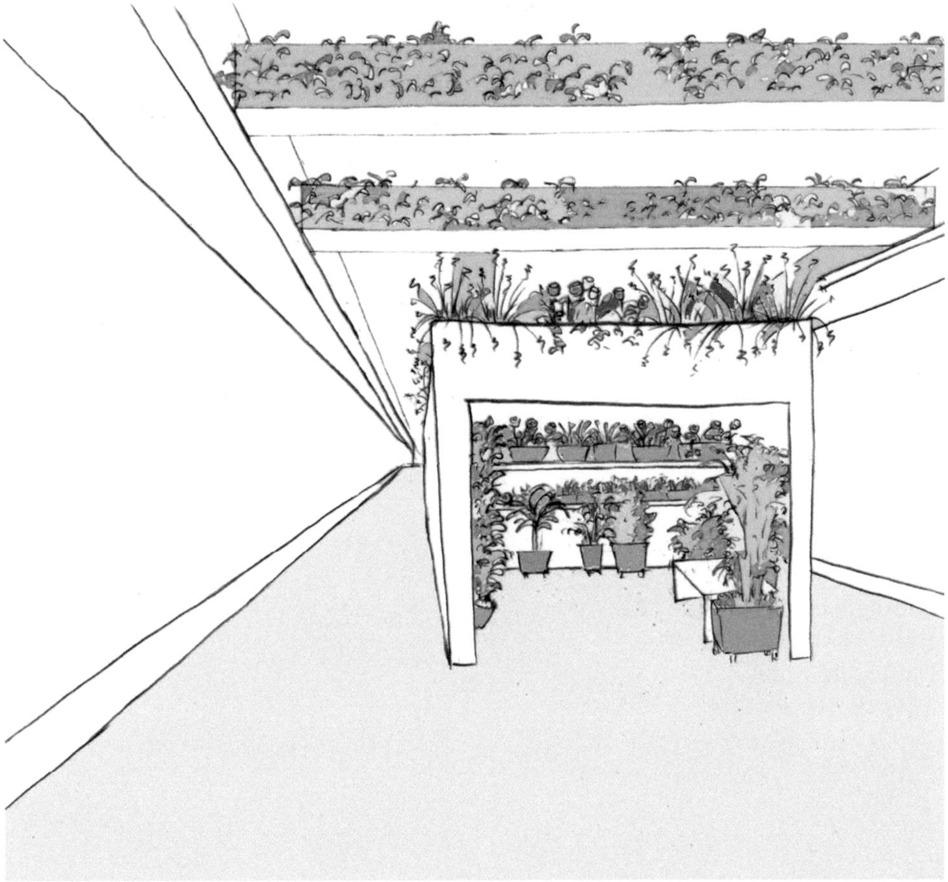

Image 2.12

Within the news stand there is a garden with benches, as well as a place for selling plants.

system and lighting system that is set on a timer. The plants in this space are grown not only on shelves designed with lights but also vertically along the walls. Though the plants are primarily for public use, sale of some of these plants may be included.

Above the news stand is also a unique place for growing plants. The plants in this area are primarily visible from the upper level though they benefit the total design and all the users of the train station.

Shallow planters with engineered soil (soil which is lighter than potting soil, used on green roofs and other sites which have weight considerations) are used on structures to reduce the weight of the planted design as necessary.

The space underneath the stairwell as well as escalator walls are opportunities for living green design. Putting plants in groups, such as those designed under the stairwells, improves the health of the plant by creating an area where the groups of plants can grow and work together for their growing benefit.

With enough smaller groups of plants under the stairwells, as well as near the seats, signage, along beams, living walls as public art, and more, the smaller designed areas of plants add up to a create a space which works together to improve the health of the users and their environment.

The benefits of reducing the infectiousness of the flu, as well as reducing air contaminants, and improving people's mental state, all illustrate reasons to include living plants in public design.

The unique spaces require knowledgeable people to maintain the site and learn the specific needs of the plants and site conditions.

Image 2.13

Gardens below the staircases and on vertical signage are opportunities for unique green designs.

Image 2.14

The train station can be seen as one large garden or a series of smaller gardens or spaces with plants to reduce the infectiousness of the airborne flu virus.

PLANTS IN THE SITE DESIGN

Plants for the train station design are chosen based on existing artificial light, as well as proposed lights for site design. The transpiration rate of the plant, the growth pattern of the leaves, including those that grow with more densely packed leaves, and plants with trichomes are what this green design specialist takes into consideration. These plants are in a train station with a temperature set at or above 70°F, as well as with a ventilation system that is set at 43% humidity or greater.

In addition to their functional needs for designing a space which reduces the infectiousness of the airborne flu virus, plants are also chosen to enhance the train station space and make it feel welcoming, healthy, and enjoyable to the site's users. There is an aesthetic balance between engaging green and an urban living planted green space (or unique urban jungle). Balancing it all is part of the reasons for the design choices.

Information on plant selections for this site is included, as well as trichome and density rates. Plants are listed from largest in scale to smaller. In Chapter 9 there is further information about the plant trichome and density rates. Further information on these plants and others can be found at www.steviefamulari.net/Famulari-Theory.

Image 2.15 *Schefflera actinophylla*, Schefflera.

Grows in zones 9–11
Has interesting palmately compound leaves.
Plant adds height and interest to a space.
Can be used to green up a large space.
Can grow in high to medium light or partial shade.
Has medium water requirements.
Height 6′–15′, spread 3′–6′.
Trichome rate 1, Density rate 7.

Image 2.15

Schefflera actinophylla, Schefflera.

Image 2.16 *Cortaderia selloana*, Pampas Grass.

Grows in zones 8–10.
Has silky plumes that add fantastic texture.
Plant adds height and movement to a room.
Plant can be used to reduce noise in a space or just to add aesthetic interest.
Can grow in high light to part shade and has medium water requirements.
Height 6′–10′, spread 4′–6′.
Trichome rate 8, Density rate 9.

Image 2.16

Cortaderia selloana, Pampas Grass.

Image 2.17 *Phoenix roebelenii*, Dwarf Date Palm.

Grows in zones 9–11.
Plant has delicate yet full texture.
Has great color and movement.
Plant will add height and a tropical feel to a space.
Can grow in high to medium light with medium water.
Height 5′–6′, spread 3′--5′.
Trichome rate 2, Density rate 8.

Image 2.17

Phoenix roebelenii, Dwarf Date Palm.

Image 2.18 *Beloperone guttata*, Shrimp Plant.

Grows in zones 9–11.
Has amazing unique flowers.
Plant adds a pop of color and curiosity to any space.
Plant used as a speciwomxn and conversation starter.
Can grow in high to medium light with low water and high humidity.
Height 2′–3′, spread 2′–3′.
Trichome rate 7, Density rate 9.

Image 2.18

Beloperone guttata, Shrimp Plant.

Image 2.19 *Columnea microphylla*, Goldfish Plant.

Grows in zones 10–11.
Has an interesting trailing growth habit.
Leaves and stems are densely covered in red hairs.
Plant used for hanging planters to add vertical interest.
Can grow in high to medium light with low water and high humidity.
Plant has unique orange flowers that are not pictured here.
Length 3′.
Trichome rate 8, Density rate 10.

Image 2.19

Columnea microphylla, Goldfish Plant.

Image 2.20 *Davallia canariensis*, Hare's Foot Fern.

- Grows in zones 10–11.
- Has exceptional roots that grow above ground and are covered in hairs.
- Plant adds a great conversation piece to any space.
- Plant used as a small speciwomxn.
- Grows best in indirect light, medium water, and high humidity.
- Height 9"–18", spread 12"–24".
- Trichome rate 10, density rate 9.

Image 2.20

Davallia canariensis, Hare's Foot Fern.

Image 2.21 *Tetrastigma voinierianum*, Chestnut vine.

- Grows in zones 10–11.
- Plant leaves are fuzzy underneath and textured on top.
- Has the ability to transform any wall or trellis into a greenwall.
- Plant used for vertical interest.
- Can grow in medium light, low water, and high humidity.
- Has a climbing vine growth habit.
- Trichome rate 7, Density rate 7.

Image 2.21

Tetrastigma voinierianum, Chestnut vine.

GREEN DESIGN SUMMARY

The details in Images 2.22 through 2.25 illustrate how living plants have been used in interior public sites in unique ways. Seating with tall plants, patterned walls with patches of plants, planted shelving with lights, and a large light fixture hanging from the ceiling inspire people to think beyond traditional potted plants or public parks planted on horizontal planes.

Lighting can be effectively applied to interior sites to address growing plants in healthy conditions. The Lowline Lab in New York City is an example of a research site which developed applied research for a park in an interior site with low light. That research illustrates that plants

Image 2.22

Interior planting with seating.

Image 2.23

Plants grown within a patterned wall.

can grow in low natural light when supplemented, and that even in enclosed spaces the humidity can be effectively addressed to have a healthy environment for both people and plants.

In public sites, some plants are designed to be visible, though not all are easily accessible for tactile access. A design for a train station includes some plants which are accessible to the public to touch, and some which are not.

In addressing the air quality of a public train station, it is beneficial to use living plants in addition to engineered systems in the design approach. Plants are known to improve air quality by adding oxygen to the air, removing harmful contaminants from the air, and adding humidity to the air. The scent of clean air is also refreshing to people.

Site-specific green design to address the plant zone, quantity of users of the site, electricity, and water sources is needed for long-term success and enjoyment of the living growing design. Additionally, the psychological benefits of being around living plants are also something notable to consider in design. Chapter 10 has further information on this topic.

In a public site, plants can be high or hanging above people's heads in order for ease of movement through the space. The maintenance and specific care of public sites, though notable, is outweighed by the health benefit to people. Not only are plants used for improving the mental health of people, but they can also be used to improve the physical health of people. In the case of the *Famulari Theory*, the living green design reduces the infectiousness of flu while also improving air quality.

The green design of this train station explores design which pushes the boundaries between interior garden and train station. To some people the function of the space – a train station – will determine how someone experiences this space. To others, the aesthetic of the design of a garden is the more important factor in how they experience the site. This design explores a balance that questions what is experienced more strongly – a train station, or a living green design such as an interior garden or unique plant conservatory. In ideal designs, these are compatible practices.

Image 2.24

Wall plants with lighting as part of the design.

Image 2.25

Chicago, Illinois, USA. Field Museum with plants in hanging mesh structure.

Chapter 3

Business Office with Open Floor Plan, Conference Room, and Small Gathering Rooms

Image 3.1

A garden design in an office setting becomes a healthy space for employees and guests.

DOI: 10.4324/9781003136880-4

EXISTING SITE INFORMATION

The company which works in this office does real estate sustainability consulting. Located in midtown Manhattan, NY, this business office has an open floor plan.

The green consulting company contains a reception area, conference room for 15 people, 1 private office, 44 desks in an open floor plan, 2 gathering rooms for 6–8 people, and a

Image 3.2

Open office design.

Image 3.3

Office entry.

Image 3.4

Office entry with guest seating.

kitchenette. The conference room is approximately 280 square feet, while the total space is approximately 1,580 square feet. In the open space, there is an average of approximately 36 square feet per person.

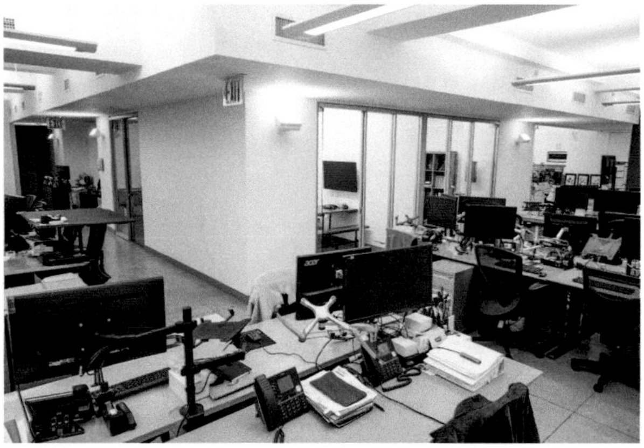

Image 3.5

Open office with small conference rooms.

A more typical office spacing is 1 person per 150 square feet. This may increase to 1 person per every 200 square feet with new guidelines. The 44 workstations/desks are in rows, all lined up next to each other. Each desk has a computer, phone, and filing cabinet. The desks are near an openable window which has a view to a street or avenue from the ninth floor. The office is typically open Monday–Friday 9am–5pm.

Image 3.6

Open office with small conference rooms.

The lighting is overhead fluorescent lighting which is not pure daylight bulbs. Some of the office lights produce a yellow light, while others produce a green light. The effects are damaging to people's eyesight in both the short and long term.

The lights are turned on in large sections with no adjustment option for one row to turn off with the others on. This tinted lighting puts undue stress on people's eyes. Poor lighting is a contributing factor to sick building syndrome (Joshi, 2008).

There are air vents throughout the space have filters which are changed according to building regulations. The air vents work to regulate the air temperature, as well as exchange air within the space. The air in this office is dry, below 30% humidity, according to readings on a few visits.

The two rooms for small meetings or having lunch do not have outside windows (Images 3.5 and 3.6). There are large glass walls for the space to feel open. Most of the walls in the spaces are painted white, with one wall a medium grey. The ceilings are high and white with florescent lighting and covered ventilation are throughout the site.

There is one conference room which can hold 10–16 people comfortably (Image 3.7), and has windows which open onto a main street. The conference room and two gathering rooms have short-pile carpet in the space. There are sources for electricity throughout the office, as well as a kitchen as a water source. A few plants in personalized pots sit on window sills on vents which give out heat, and dry the plants out quickly.

Image 3.7

Large conference room.

Image 3.8

Open office plan.

Image 3.9

The office space has a design of plants at sitting height, standing height, and above standing height. The totality of the gardens creates a space which can help reduce the airborne flu virus.

GREEN DESIGN SOLUTION

Multiple plants and other design approaches are used in the redesign of the office space to reduce the spread of the infectiousness of the airborne flu virus as well as to improve the design of the office for SBS. These include:

- Moveable planters with wheels between desks for plants and humidifier to reduce the infectiousness of the airborne flu virus
- Adding plants above huwomxn height near the ceiling to reduce the infectiousness of the airborne flu virus
- UV lights within the water system to reduce the infectiousness of the airborne flu virus
- Use desks which are designed to have monitor lifts so that the screens can lower below the desk for a cleaner, more open design
- Lighting of daylight bulbs for each set of desks and plants to increase the plants' ability to live and grow, as well as for reducing the effects of sick building syndrome (SBS) (further information on SBS can be found in Chapter 10)
- Changing the temperature and humidity settings of the office ventilation to reduce the infectiousness of the airborne flu virus, as well as for reducing the effects of SBS
- The addition of plants for reducing the soundwaves a few decibels through the open office for reducing the effects of SBS (further information on this in Chapter 7)

Image 3.10

The office entry has a vertical garden as well as a mobile planter and a humidifier and lights. Plants are also hanging from the ceiling.

- Adding an activated carbon filter to the planters to be effective in improving the air quality for contaminants such as formaldehyde, benzene, ammonia, trichloroethylene, xylene, alcohols, and acetone as well as dust and allergens for reducing the effects of SBS as well as producing fresher air (further information on activated carbon filters in the restaurant Chapter 4)

The rectangular planters between the desks have a mix of plants as well as humidifiers, a UV light within the water system, and a pump for the circulating water. The frame of the planter is built with wheels for mobility, and has space for multiple plants to grow and thrive. The aesthetic of the planter's base can be based on the artist's choice – including words, tiles, sculptural elements, colors, or other choices.

The planter has wire supports at the top to help with plants which may need structural support. The humidifier in the planter is beneficial for adding humidity to the immediate area near the plants and employees, as well as affecting the larger office space for humidity. The UV light disinfects the water in the planter of viruses and bacteria which may get into the water.

The planters are designed to have an activated carbon filter within the built structure. One existing system which uses an activated carbon filter in a planter is the Plant Air Purifier® system.

> The Plant Air Purifier system pulls air down through the growth media where the air pollutants are captured by activated carbon. The activated carbon and pebbles have porous surfaces that hold the pollutants in place, allowing microbes in the root zone to break them down into components that both the plant and themselves can digest. Thus, the Plant Air Purifier is bioregenerative (self-cleaning) and there are no filters to replace.
>
> **(Plant Air Purifier, 2016)**

Moveable planters are in the shared open space as well as in the large conference room and smaller gathering rooms. In the smaller gathering rooms there are additional greenwalls with multiple plants, creating a space for people to review works or have a moment of quiet or eat lunch in a room with fresh air and a green design.

The locations of these mobile planters, as well as the greenwalls and planted areas of the conference rooms and other spaces, are intentionally spaced to be within six feet of where employees are sitting. This six-foot distance for living plants and humidity is for reducing the infectiousness of the airborne flu virus from an initial cough or sneeze.

Image 3.11

Vertical gardens with planters at varying heights along the wall.

Additional plants that are included in the office space design are used for the many droplets of the airborne virus that are in the air and can be reduced in infectiousness with the application of the multiple parts of the *Famulari Theory*.

Throughout the office there are vents near the windows as well as high on the walls and on the ceiling. The ventilation system regulates the heating, cooling, humidity, and air exchange rate. Adjusting the settings of the vents to increase the humidity to 43% minimum as well as a temperature of 70°F or higher is required for this design.

Lighting for each unit of desks can be turned on or off while not affecting the other lights of the office. The lights are daylight bulbs, 5,600–6,000°K (Kelvin), allowing for full-spectrum lighting which is beneficial for the eyes. Additionally, full-spectrum lighting is beneficial in reducing the effects of SBS. Changing the lighting is one approach to improving the effects of SBS in the office. Further information about SBS is discussed in Chapter 10. Changing the lights allows for some areas of the office to have lights on while others are off. Plant lights can be scheduled on a timer to be turned on for select hours to help the plants grow and thrive in the office space, with daylight bulbs which are beneficial for the health of the people and plants.

The irrigation for the plants near the ceiling is designed to work in zones. Each zone, similar to the desk planter, can be on a timer for watering. The tank for the water is located on the floor with water pumped to the plants near the ceiling. Catch systems are in place for the interior irrigation of planters and greenwalls to address any water overflow.

Image 3.12

The office space can be seen as one large garden or a series of garden areas. The plants add color, scent, humidity, and can help reduce the airborne flu virus.

Image 3.13

The conference room has planters on the ground to allow an open area for people to gather for presentations.

Image 3.14

The smaller conference rooms have a garden which can also be for individuals to sit for a moment to gather their thoughts.

Plants in the office space also act to absorb sound through their leaves. Plants reduce the sound waves that travel through the open office space as the leaves absorb some of the sound waves. With the large open space of this style of office, reducing the myriad of sounds is beneficial for all users of the space.

Using a diversity of plants is beneficial for the space. In interior spaces, one reason for diversity is to have different plants which remove different pollutants from the air. In exterior spaces diverse plants also improve the soil, water, and ecosystem. Aesthetically, having multiple plants which are compatible in style, color, shape, form, and scent is pleasing for the users of the space.

This living green design requires knowledgeable maintenance, as do most spatial designs. Generally, fine tuning and maintenance for this green office are more frequent during the first few months and years as the plants become acclimated to their site and conditions, as well as early in the warm and cold season after determining how often people open the windows (high-rise buildings typically do not have openable windows).

After early fine tuning of the watering system and lights, maintenance would include weekly checking of the plants for growth, adding water to the planters, wiring new plant growth to the support wires as needed, checking and adding nutrition to the soil as needed, removing dead leaves or branches, and replacing plants as they grow too large for the pots or space.

PLANTS IN THE SITE DESIGN

Plants for the office design are chosen based on the natural light of the office, the existing artificial light, the proposed plant lights for the office design, the transpiration rate of the plant, the growth pattern of the leaves – including those that grow with more densely packed leaves, and plants with trichomes. These plants are in an office with a temperature set at or above 70°F, as well as with a ventilation system that is set at 43% humidity or greater. The location of the plants in relation to the windows as well as the ventilation is necessary to know in order to put plants in ideal conditions to grow.

In addition to the functional needs for designing a space which reduces the infectiousness of the airborne flu virus, plants are also chosen to enhance the office space and make it feel welcoming, healthy, and enjoyable to the employees. There is an aesthetic balance between engaging green and office lush garden. Balancing it all is one of the reasons for the design choices.

Information on plant selections for this site is included, as well as trichome and density rates. Plants are listed from largest in scale to smaller. In Chapter 9 there is further information about the plant trichome and density rates. Further information on these plants and others can be found at www.steviefamulari.net/Famulari-Theory.

Image 3.15 *Dracaena marginata*, Dragon Tree.

- Grows in zones 10–12.
- Adds texture and height to a room.
- Plant used as an interesting accent to soften the space.
- Can grow in high to medium light, and requires medium water and humidity.
- Height 6′, spread 3′.
- Trichome rate 1, Density rate 8.

Image 3.15

Dracaena marginata, Dragon Tree.

Image 3.16 *Pelargonium capitatum*, Rose Geranium.

Grows in zones 8–11.
Plant adds a welcome pop of color to any space.
Emits a rose scent when the stems are disturbed.
Plant used for accent, color, and enjoyment.
Can grow in high light and requires medium water.
Height 2′, spread 2′.
Trichome rate 8, Density rate 9.

Image 3.16

Pelargonium capitatum, Rose Geranium.

Image 3.17 *Kohleria amabilis*, Tree Gloxinia.

Grows in zones 8–11.
Has brightly colored impressive flowers.
Plant adds an interesting focal point to a space.
Can grow in indirect light to light shade.
Plant requires medium water.
Height 12″-24″.
Trichome rate 8, Density rate 7.

Image 3.17

Kohleria amabilis, Tree Gloxinia.

Image 3.18 *Kalanchoe tomentosa*, Panda Plant.

Grows in zones 10–12.
Plant has a fantastic fuzzy texture.
Has an attractive stiff growth habit.
Can grow in high light to partial shade.
Requires low water and medium to low humidity.
Height 12″–24″, spread 12″–24″.
Trichome rate 9, Density rate 9.

Image 3.18

Kalanchoe tomentosa, Panda Plant.

Image 3.19 *Alsobia dianthiflora*, Lace Flower.

Grows in zones 9–10.
Plant has interesting furry white flowers.
Looks great when allowed to spill over the edge of its container.
Grows best in high light with medium water and humidity.
Can grow well in artificial lighting.
Height 4″–6″, spread 12″–18″.
Trichome rate 8, Density rate 10.

Image 3.19

Alsobia dianthiflora, Lace Flower.

Image 3.20 *Saxifraga stolonifera*, Strawberry Begonia.

Grows in zones 6–9.
Plant has rounded leaves and with interesting coloration.
It sends out runners adding an attractive hanging aspect.
Plant produces unique flowers pictured here.
Can grow in high light and partial shade.
Plant requires high water and humidity.
Height 3″–6″, spread 12″–24″.
Trichome rate 8, Density rate 8.

Image 3.20

Saxifraga stolonifera, Strawberry Begonia.

Image 3.21 *Epipremnum aureum*, Golden Pothos.

Grows in zones 10–12.
Has thick glossy heart-shaped leaves.
Plant can be cut to stay dense or left alone to grow long.
Likes low light and low water.
Plant is easy to grow with little care and adapts well to most spaces.
Length 6′–10′.
Trichome rate 1, Density rate 7.

Image 3.21

Epipremnum aureum, Golden Pothos.

GREEN DESIGN SUMMARY

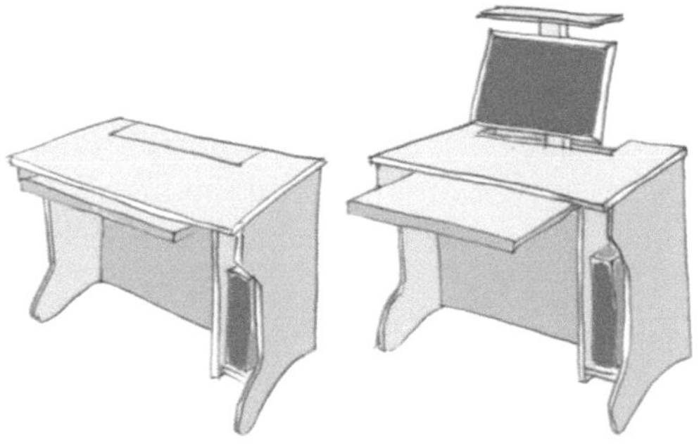

Image 3.22

Office desk which has a monitor lift in order to be able to use the desk space while hiding the monitor.

Multiple elements of the office design already exist. An example (Image 3.22) is that desks which have monitors that lift and lower are available in single desks and double desks, as well as with wheelchair access. Using these desks allows employees to not continually have a monitor in their eyeline as the primary focus of the desk, and allows more space for reading and analyzing papers, and other activities. It also allows neighboring employees to use the desk space when it is available.

Reducing the flu virus improves an employee's health and their overall performance at work, which can help balance off the long-term costs of the living green design. Some offices have designs in space with living plants of different scales, shapes, and heights throughout the office. In Image 3.23, the office has plants both in the shared space as well as in the cubicle area, while Image 3.24 illustrates a business with plants framed on the walls.

Image 3.23

Office with plants throughout the space.

Image 3.24

Wall with planters as colorfully framed artworks.

The plants serve multiple beneficial roles. These include the psychological benefits of enjoying plants around you, the improved productivity of employees, absorbing sounds in a large open space, and improving air quality.

Reducing the flu virus improves an employee's health and their overall performance at work which can balance the long-term costs of the living green design.

As a green aesthetic this office design pushes the boundaries between an interior garden and an open office. Some users will see this space as a garden that people can work in, while others will see it as a green office. For the *Famulari Theory* application the plants are placed near the users. As an aesthetic, plants are designed to grow with a loose natural shape, and over time the plants weave through the shapes of the space, growing and changing in unique magical ways.

REFERENCES

Joshi, S. M. (2008). The sick building syndrome. *Indian Journal of Occupational and Environmental Medicine, 12*(2), 61–64. doi:10.4103/0019-5278.43262

Plant Air Purifier. (2016). U.S. Health Equipment Company, Inc. https://www.plantairpurifier.com/product_benefits_-_overview.html (retrieved 4 December 2020).

Chapter 4

Restaurant – Interior, Multiple Tables, and Layouts

Image 4.1

The restaurant design has plants at multiple heights, as well as with a variety of plants and mobile planters to allow the design to be versatile and effective for reducing the airborne flu virus.

DOI: 10.4324/9781003136880-5

EXISTING SITE INFORMATION

The restaurant chapter explores interior restaurant layouts with varying lighting. Unlike the other five design chapters which focus on one specific site, this chapter uses multiple different restaurant sites as design examples with living green solutions.

Image 4.2

Restaurant with large windows and high sunlight through the space.

Restaurants are unique designs in that they are spaces which have constant turnover and change. Tables are re-arranged frequently to account for different sized events and gatherings. This versatility is a necessity for this type of business.

Image 4.3

Restaurant with high natural sunlight in some spaces and artificial lighting in others.

Restaurants vary in their opening hours. Daytime through nighttime hours, some open late into the night, can be expected. Additionally, employees arrive before customers for set up, and stay afterwards for cleaning. This means that the space has multiple changing people in it for extended hours.

Lighting plays an important role in enhancing the atmosphere of the space. The lighting, both existing sunlight and artificial light,

Image 4.4

Restaurant with high sunlight in one area of the space.

is designed to create a mood in which people are comfortable to eat, talk, and gather. Using both lighting to enhance the restaurant, while also using correct lighting for living green plants is needed for applying the *Famulari Theory*.

Some tables are located near doors which open and close to the street, some tables are near windows which may or may not open, while other tables are in secluded semi-private spaces without windows or doors nearby. The great variety of locations means designing different styles of spaces where people are comfortable with different lighting and settings.

Sounds from the gathering of people talking and moving as well as from outside the windows and doors are all

Image 4.5

Restaurant with no direct sunlight in this part of the space.

considered when designing a restaurant. Acoustics to dampen sound for semi-privacy, as well as to enhance sounds from live performers or sound systems, are important to consider. Going to a restaurant is not only for the food, drinks, and events at the establishment but for the great company and dialogue with your friends. Having fantastic conversations and events that stay with you for years to come means creating a space where people can hear the people at their table while not fully hearing the conversations of nearby table guests.

Image 4.6

Restaurant with mixed natural sunlight and artificial light through the space.

In addition to sound, scent plays an important role in a positive experience at a restaurant. Restaurants have a myriad of food options and have a myriad of smells which emanate from the kitchen as well as the tables filled with foods. Making sure the scents are appealing and not overwhelming means having clean vents and good air circulation.

Image 4.7

Restaurant with multiple areas of low sunlight.

Cleaning of the space is daily, with cleaners, some with chemicals and some natural, used on different surfaces. The chemical cleaners produce contaminants in the air which can be circulated and filtered with ventilation systems as well as with living plants.

Contaminants from the outdoor air also can play a role in restaurants. Windows and doors may be open frequently throughout the year allowing outdoor air to mix with indoor air. Generally, this is a wanted feature, allowing fresh outdoor air to improve the indoor air. When restaurants are bordered by their own parking lot, the air from the parking lot with car exhaust contaminants can affect the indoor air negatively. Locating the parking so it cannot be viewed from the window is not only for visual appeal but also for the indoor air quality. Plants can help to address pollutants from cars for restaurants where this may be applicable.

Image 4.8

Restaurant with a garden on the ground plane, the eye plane, and the overhead plane. While some columns of plants are mobile and self-contained with wheels and irrigation, other parts of the design are built into the space.

GREEN DESIGN SOLUTION

Multiple plants, water features, and lighting are used in the redesign of the restaurant to reduce the spread of the infectiousness of the airborne flu virus as well as to create an atmosphere of living green design. These include:

- Moveable planters with wheels between tables for plants and a humidifier to reduce the infectiousness of the airborne flu virus
- Planted, non-moveable screens, and walls to act as air filters for reducing the airborne flu virus as well as to absorb soundwaves and create semi-privacy
- Adding plants above huwomxn height near the ceiling to reduce the infectiousness of the airborne flu virus
- Water features to create light pleasant sounds while also adding some humidity to the air in the space
- UV lights within the water system to reduce the infectiousness of the airborne flu virus
- Lighting of small daylight bulbs for some of the living green planted areas to increase the plants' ability to live and grow well
- Changing the temperature and humidity settings of the restaurant ventilation to reduce the infectiousness of the airborne flu virus

Image 4.9

Planters are on the tables as well as hanging at varying heights from the beams.

- The addition of plants for reducing the soundwaves through the open restaurant (see courtyard Chapter 7 for further information on soundwaves)
- Adding an activated carbon filter to the planters to effectively improve the air quality for contaminants such as formaldehyde, benzene, ammonia, trichloroethylene, xylene, alcohols, and acetone as well as dust and allergens for producing fresher air

Plants are designed into the restaurant spaces from the floor all the way up to the ceiling. The varying heights of plants and humidity are considered in their locations to address the myriad sizes of the airborne flu virus and other contaminants moving through the air. The intentional use of plants at multiple heights helps to remove the flu virus and other contaminants as the air circulates throughout the different heights.

In order for the green design to live and be effective, the ventilation and heating systems of the restaurants must be set to not go below 70°F and to maintain a minimum of 43% humidity. The applied *Famulari Theory* green design can supplement the existing heating and ventilation systems in the sites.

Similar to offices, restaurants have moving tables and therefore need moving planters. The larger moving planters can be on wheels with plants, lighting, structure to hold the plants as they grow, irrigation with pump and tubing, a humidifier, a UV light, and an activated carbon filter.

Image 4.10

Movable planters on wheels include a plant light, UV light for cleaning water, activated carbon filter, water pumps, humidifier, planter sloped for water drainage, and water containers.

In addition to the plant design used for reducing the airborne flu virus, the activated carbon filter removes airborne pollutants common in indoor air. In both commercial and residential sites airborne contaminants include VOCs, formaldehyde, benzene, ammonia, trichloroethylene, xylene, alcohols, and acetone. Dust and allergens are also found airborne in commercial and residential sites. Activated carbon filters are able to reduce these contaminants.

Large-scale greenwalls and water features add color and a soothing background sound to the rooms. The water features designed for the walls also add humidity to the room which helps for ease of breathing as well as applying the *Famulari Theory* to the site. UV lights are added to the water systems to clean the viruses in the water. UV lights are designed to not be seen by people and serve a vital function in cleaning water.

These designed living walls are not meant to move and have planters added to the structure. The plants in these design sites not only help to improve the air quality by reducing the infectiousness of the airborne flu virus but also help to reduce the sound waves throughout the space. Sound waves are diffused by the loose soft leaves and gaps of space between them. This can be beneficial in large open spaces with multiple people talking at the same time. (Further information on sound waves can be found in the courtyard Chapter 7.)

Planters are added to non-movable screens. The living planted screens create an atmosphere with vertical gardens throughout the space. Lights are added to the screens to give the plants suitable light to grow. The LED plant lights can change colors if needed; however, they are also set on a timer which is suitable for the plants for their growth.

LED lights can be designed into a water feature and green walls as well as where plants are throughout the space. The LED lights are for plant growth as well as for creating interesting atmospheres. Lights can change to different color temperatures (daylight white through warm white, purples, blues, green, etc.) and brightness. There are apps for phones which can be used to change the LED lights in an instant or by a timer. More importantly, LED lights may be needed in order for the plants to have a healthy lifespan and growth.

In the examples of the green designs of the restaurant, the lighting varies from full direct sunlight to no visible sunlight. When spaces do not have daylight, plants can be still be added to a site with the addition of artificial lights. In cases where there is sunlight and mixed light (some sunlight and some artificial lights), putting plants in lighting which best suits them is considered in the design.

Designing a space with plants at different heights is a benefit to the design of these garden restaurants. Plants are placed at the ground level, the sitting height, standing height, and above

Image 4.11

Floor-to-ceiling water features and greenwalls are designed into the space, allowing for mobility of the tables.

Image 4.12

The metal dividers are designed into greenwalls with planters and LED lights at varying heights.

Image 4.13

The design has floor-to-ceiling plant materials with both stationary and movable planters. The primary focus of the plants is the ceiling plant design.

standing height (ceiling height). The circulating air has more opportunity to be in contact with a plant when there are multiple plants are varying heights and locations throughout a space.

Both movable planters and permanent structures for plants are designed to create long-term stability of plants as well as flexibility to rearrange a space for different events. Water features add needed humidity to large spaces while UV lights designed into the water feature clean the water of contaminants, bacteria, and viruses which may get into the water system.

PLANTS IN THE SITE DESIGN

Plants for the restaurant design are chosen based on the natural light of the restaurant, the existing artificial light, the proposed plant lights for the restaurant design, the transpiration rate of the plant, and the growth pattern of the leaves – including those that grow with more densely packed leaves, and plants with trichomes. These plants are in a restaurant with a temperature set at or above 70°F, as well as with a ventilation system that is set at 43% humidity or greater. With the doors and windows of the restaurant opening frequently, the range of temperatures is also considered.

In addition to the functional needs of designing a space which reduces the infectiousness of the airborne flu virus, plants are also chosen to enhance the office space and make it feel welcoming, healthy, and enjoyable to the employees and guests. There is an aesthetic balance between engaging green and restaurant jungle. Balancing it all is one of the reasons for the design choices.

Information on plant selections for this site is included, as well as trichome and density rates. Plants are listed from largest in scale to smaller. In Chapter 9 there is further information about the plant trichome and density rates. Further information on these plants and others can be found at www.steviefamulari.net/Famulari-Theory.

Image 4.14 *Chamaedorea seifrizii,* Bamboo Palm.

- Grows in zones 10–11.
- Plant has a large impressive presence.
- Gives any space a tropical feel.
- Plant can be used as a speciwomxn piece.
- Grows best with medium light, water, and humidity.
- Height 4′–10′, spread 3′–5′.
- Trichome rate 1, Density rate 8.

Image 4.14

Chamaedorea seifrizii, Bamboo Palm.

Image 4.15 *Coleus amboinicus*, Cuban Oregano.

- Grows in zones 9–11.
- Leaves have an oregano-like scent and fantastic texture.
- Plant used for greening up a space and fits nicely on the rolling trays.
- Grows best with medium light and water.
- Height 1′–3′, spread 2′–4′.
- Trichome rate 7, Density rate 8.

Image 4.15

Coleus amboinicus, Cuban Oregano.

Image 4.16 *Spathiphyllum wallisii*, Peace Lily.

- Grows in zones 11–12.
- Has fantastic dark green leaves with a nice texture.
- Plant has interesting white flowers on long stalks.
- Can grow in indirect bright light to part shade.
- Grows best with medium water and high humidity.
- Height 1′–2′, spread 1′–2′.
- Trichome rate 1, Density rate 8.

Image 4.16

Spathiphyllum wallisii, Peace Lily.

Image 4.17 *Schizanthus pinnatus*, Poor Man's Orchid.

- Grows in zones 2–11.
- Has beautiful interesting flowers.
- Plant adds cheerful pops of color to interior spaces.
- Can grow in high light to partial shade.
- Plant has medium water requirements.
- Height 12″–18″, spread 9″–12″.
- Trichome rate 7, Density rate 8.

Image 4.17

Schizanthus pinnatus, Poor Man's Orchid.

Image 4.18 *Maranta leuconeura* "Kerchoveana," Prayer Plant.

- Grows in zones 11–12.
- Has gorgeous leaves with an interesting pattern.
- Plant leaves will fold up when left in the dark for about 15 minutes.
- Plant thrives with high indirect light.
- Requires medium water and high humidity.
- Height 6″–12″, spread 6″–24″.
- Trichome rate 1, Density rate 8.

Image 4.18

Maranta leuconeura "Kerchoveana," Prayer Plant.

Image 4.19 *Columnea gloriosa*, Goldfish Plant.

- Grows in zones 11–12.
- Has bright unique flowers.
- Leaves have great texture and flow from hanging baskets.
- Plant likes high to medium light.
- Has high water and humidity requirements.
- Image shown is a purple leaf variety, it also comes in a green leaf variety, length 3′.
- Trichome rate 8, Density rate 9.

Image 4.19

Columnea gloriosa, Goldfish Plant.

Image 4.20 *Sempervivum* "Rococo," Hen and Chicks.

- Grows in zones 10–11.
- Has great color and texture.
- Plant can be used to add interest to small spaces.
- Plant has low water requirements.
- Grows well in high light and part shade.
- Height 6″, spread 8″.
- Trichome rate 8, Density rate 10.

Image 4.20

Sempervivum "Rococo," Hen and Chicks.

GREEN DESIGN SUMMARY

Each restaurant is unique not only in its menu of food, but also in location, atmosphere, hours, lighting, sound, materials, and much more. The uniqueness of each site can be an asset in designing a healthy green space that is site-specific and considers the design aesthetics of the owners. This can lead to more success for the business.

Images 4.21 through 4.23 illustrate some of the creative ways interior and exterior sites have used their vertical space to create gardens with living plants, patterns, colors, textures, shapes, and materials. Living vertical garden designs can be playful through uniform, vibrant in colors through subtle, large throughout a space, or smaller in scale. The variety of styles and options in design is as open as the designers themselves.

Image 4.21

Café with planter boxes along the wall of windows.

Image 4.22

Wall with plants designed into the pattern. The plants can be changed as wanted.

Creating spaces where living green plants are used as a notable part of the space is beneficial for employees as well as users in both the short and long term. With a developed weekly maintenance plan, these unique interior gardens can grow for many years.

Image 4.23

Living plant wall with a pattern.

Chapter 5

House – Living Room, Kitchen, Dining Room, Office, and Bedroom

Image 5.1

Each room of the house has its own garden with plants and water features inspiring each room to have different effects while reducing the infectiousness of the airborne flu.

DOI: 10.4324/9781003136880-6

EXISTING SITE INFORMATION

This house is located on City Island, an area in the Bronx, NY.

The house residents include a married couple, 2 children between 9 and 14 years old, a dog, and cat. The first floor is approximately 860 square feet total, with the living room and entry being 468 square feet, the kitchen at 225 square feet, and the dining room at 110 square feet. On the second floor, the main bedroom is approximately 240 square feet, and the office is 200 square feet. There is also a children's bedroom and bathroom on the second floor.

The house entry is a gathering space where people put on or take off their coats and shoes, or put items from the day. During the summer, the front door is left open with a

Image 5.2

Living room in a two-story house.

Image 5.3

Entry to house.

Image 5.4
Living room with bay window, fireplace, and ceiling fan.

screen, allowing air from the outside to come into the house easily. The ceiling fan in the living room is used for air circulation. The living room is the gathering space for watching television as well as where the children's friends gather to play games or watch movies.

This family has guests of different ages in the house throughout the day during all times of the year. The front door and back door are opened throughout the day for the dog to enjoy the outdoors as well as for the family and guests to freely flow through the space.

The use of the house as an office or classroom has become increasingly common in recent times. Entire rooms or parts of rooms are adjusted to allow the space to be more effective for teaching, learning, office work, meetings, research, art, exercise, and more. In some cases, the rooms serve multiple purposes during different times of the day or week.

In this household, most shared rooms currently double as offices with desks for one or more members of the family while they work from home. The living room has one desk for a family member to use for working at home during the day, and other rooms have additional desks and work spaces.

The rooms have sealed wood floors throughout the house, with the exception of the bathrooms with tiled floors. The house is cleaned each month by a professional cleaner who uses cleaners with chemicals. The pets are free to roam and play throughout the house. Plants are growing in some rooms of the house with care by the family on a routine basis. Some plants are moved outdoors in the summer, and moved indoors from autumn through spring.

The house is heated by a gas furnace with heating through base boards in the house. The upstairs and downstairs areas can be set to different temperatures. The temperature is typically set at a minimum of 70°F or above. The cooling system is through forced air in the vents in the ceiling of each room. There is no control for the humidity. The filter is changed yearly.

Image 5.5

Kitchen.

The dining room and kitchen are connected in the space. There are double sliding doors to the deck and backyard from the dining room and kitchen and common area. The table in the dining room can sit eight people at the main table, with additional seating at the kitchen island.

The dining room used to be used primarily for meals. In recent months, one member of the family sometimes takes the space of the dining room table to work from home, and uses the table during the day. Additionally, there is a small desk near the sliding doors for one of the children to do schoolwork.

Image 5.6

Dining room.

The kitchen island is a place of gathering throughout the day. It is where food is prepared, snacks are enjoyed, lunch gatherings are held for the family and friends of the family, and people hang out to have a drink and talk while meals are prepared. It is one of the main gathering spaces during the active hours of the house, along with the living room.

On the second floor, off the hallway there is a main bedroom which has windows for cross-ventilation, as well as a ceiling fan.

The two children share a bedroom. Friends of the boys come to hang out and play in the children's bedroom as well as in the office.

The office has a large three-panel window and an additional window for ventilation. The desk has space for two people to work, as well one huwomxn to read in a comfortable chair. There is a closet for the storage of office supplies. Additionally, one of the adult members of the house uses this space for work when it is not in use by one or more of the children and their friends.

Image 5.7

Main bedroom.

Image 5.8

Home office.

Image 5.9

The living room has planters on wheels across the floor as well as a vertical planter, water feature, and plants at higher levels. The living room garden is a versatile space for changes throughout the seasons.

GREEN DESIGN SOLUTION

Multiple plants and other design approaches are used in improving the house to reduce the spread of the infectiousness of the airborne flu virus for the homeowners as well as the guests. These include:

- Putting large planters on wheels for ease of movement during events, as well as during flu season to create more impact on a specific room when needed
- Adding humidifiers and water features in plant corners and greenwalls
- Adding plants combined with unique light fixtures near the ceiling as well as within desks lamps to reduce the infectiousness of the airborne flu virus
- UV lights within the water system to reduce the infectiousness of the airborne flu virus
- Changing to household cleaners with natural disinfectants to improve the air quality and allow the plants to address the other airborne contaminants
- Lighting of daylight bulbs for all areas where plants are, as well as throughout the house to increase the plants' ability to live and grow
- Continuing to use the temperature setting of 70°F or above in all seasons to reduce the infectiousness of the airborne flu virus

Image 5.10

Living room with moveable floor planters, greenwalls, water features, and lights.

- The addition of plants for adding oxygen in bedrooms at night for improving overall health and comfort
- Adding an activated carbon filter to the planters to be effective in improving the air quality for contaminants such as formaldehyde, benzene, ammonia, trichloroethylene, xylene, alcohols, and acetone as well as dust and allergens – all of which are found in the furniture throughout the house

The living room of the house has plants added to the sitting corner, the desk area, near the couches, and with hanging planter design. Living greenwalls placed high on the walls are an alternative to hanging planters from the ceiling.

Planters on rollers, some with an activated carbon filter, and a humidifier in the plant corner are used in this design (further information on carbon filters can be found in the restaurant Chapter 4). Planters on the floor are placed on rollers to allow ease of movement when arranging for events or for moving to create a corner for a house member with the flu to work and relax in.

All desks in the house have their own light stand, with a planter built into the light stand as part of the design. This allows each member of the family to have their own desk plant

Image 5.11

The dining room garden has a light fixture designed with plants as well as a gallery of plants along the wall. This garden can have mixed seasonal plants as well as long-term plants for reducing the airborne flu virus.

which will have the benefit of the lamp light with the daylight bulb in it. The plants within the desk lamps can be cut back as they grow larger than their container. The cutting may be used in other parts of the home. One benefit of plants is that with their growth, new plants can be propagated so a larger garden can be grown over time, or if space does not permit this, the new growth can be shared with friends to expand the benefits of greening with plants.

The dining room is connected to the kitchen. The combined space allows the design with plants to flow from one area to the next. In the dining room there are three important areas for plants where people are working – the light fixture with plants above the table, the living wall with plants and a humidifier, and the plants by the sliding door.

The light fixture is redesigned with plants as part of the structure. The plants in this structure can receive a subtle heat from the daylight bulbs and proximity to the light fixture. This is accounted for when choosing plants. A combination of plants with loose vining growth which can weave through the structure is used. Plants which are able to help reduce the infectiousness of the airborne flu virus are used to help with the small virus droplets which are floating and moving through the air after coughs and sneezes.

The living wall in the dining room also has a humidifier built into it which helps to keep the humidity above 43% in the colder seasons as well as during the warmer seasons when the air conditioning system is turned on.

The sliding double doors add much light to the space, though only one door is used for going onto the deck. Hanging plants of varying sizes can act as a filter of light and semi-privacy in this space. As one or two members of the household use this area with a desk and the dining room table, creating a colorful hanging plant design in front of one door can add to the totality to connect the design and improve air quality and allow the floor space to be altered with more ease.

As a frequent gathering space for the family and guests, the kitchen has two major areas for green design. The first is the light fixture over the island. The lights are changed to daylight bulbs and plants are designed with a light fixture. The second is the shelves and cabinet by the *window which have plants with trichomes.*

Similar to the dining room, the light fixture above the island is an opportunity for creativity and design fun. Intertwining plants within a light structure which hangs from the ceiling is

Image 5.12

The kitchen garden has plants designed into the light fixture and smaller nooks for plants as the island is a common gathering place for the family.

Image 5.13

The bedroom garden has plants which produce oxygen at night as well as those which add humidity to reduce the infectiousness of the airborne flu virus.

interesting because the light fixture gives the plant a structure to grow around and give shape to the plant growth. The light fixture with daylight bulbs may also add some subtle heat to the potted plant. Between the sunlight and artificial light, this planted area may have multiple plants which bloom throughout the year.

By the window there are shelves which contain plants as well as hanging plants from the ceiling. When cooking, people use the sink, stove, and countertops – all of which are by the window. The window is designed with plants with trichomes. With the sink and dishwasher, humidity is not the primary focus of these plants.

The living garden design for the bedroom includes plants for the reduction of the infectiousness of the flu, as well as plants which produce oxygen throughout the night for when people are sleeping. (More information about plants which produce oxygen at night is in Chapter 9.) Plants near the bed are for both functions. Along with a humidifier, the plants which are not directly near the bed are for increasing the humidity in the room.

The layers of improving health with the use of plants in a bedroom include improved overnight breathing, psychological health, and reduction of the infectiousness of the airborne flu virus.

Image 5.14

The home office garden has the majority of the plants along the wall behind the desk. A ceiling fan for air circulation is needed to circulate the air to the plants for filtering the air contaminants.

Creating a garden for the bedroom includes vertical greening. In homes there are many people moving through the space. Using the vertical surfaces is an asset in green design with plants for all the users of the space.

A comfortable reading chair is placed near a corner of plants and a wall of green plants with a humidifier. The person who is sitting in the chair is surrounded by plants, with daylight bulbs, while sitting at a comfortable temperature and humidity.

There are additional plants on the desk. The desk plants add to the totality of the green office design and are beneficial for reducing flu infectiousness when people who are near the computers cough or sneeze. The plants can hold the airborne huwomxn flu virus on the leaf surface without being harmed or without needing cleaning. Air circulation moves the remainder of the airborne virus out the open window, or over to the wall and corner of multiple plants.

Creating a space for the adults, teenagers, and friends of the family to work, study, attend school from the house, is the focus of the living green home office design

PLANTS IN THE SITE DESIGN

Plants for the home are chosen based on the natural light, the existing artificial lights, the proposed lights for the space, the transpiration rate of the plant, and the growth pattern of the leaves – including those that grow with more densely packed leaves, and plants with trichomes. These plants are in a house with a temperature set at or above 70°F, as well as with a ventilation system that is set at 43% humidity or greater. A diverse set of plants is used in this house design.

In addition to their functional needs for designing a space which reduces the infectiousness of the airborne flu virus, plants are also chosen to enhance the home and make it feel welcoming, healthy, and enjoyable to the family and friends. There is an aesthetic balance between engaging green and home jungle. Balancing it all is one of the reasons for the design choices.

Information on plant selections for this site is included, as well as trichome and density rates. Plants are listed from largest in scale to smaller. In Chapter 9 there is further information about the plant trichome and density rates. Further information on these plants and others can be found at www.steviefamulari.net/Famulari-Theory.

Image 5.15 *Chrysalidocarpus lutescens*, Areca Palm.

- Grows in zones 9–11.
- Gives the interior space a tropical feel.
- Plant has a delicate texture that can soften the corner of any room.
- Can grow in high indirect light to part shade.
- Prefers medium water and high humidity.
- Height 6′–12′, spread 6′–8′.
- Trichome rate 1, Density rate 8.

Image 5.15

Chrysalidocarpus lutescens, Areca Palm.

Image 5.16 *Musa acuminata* "Dwarf Cavendish," Dwarf Cavendish Banana.

- Grows in zones 10–11.
- Has large thick leaves with excellent texture.
- Plant transforms any room into a green space.
- Plant used as a speciwomxn plant.
- Grows best in high light with medium water.
- Height 4′–6′.
- Trichome rate 1, Density rate 8.

Image 5.16

Musa acuminata "Dwarf Cavendish," Dwarf Cavendish Banana.

Image 5.17 *Tibouchina urvilleana*, Princess Flower.

- Grows in zones 9–11.
- Has gorgeous purple flowers.
- Plant has super soft leaves that are impossible not to touch.
- Plant adds great color and texture to a home.
- Grows well with high light and medium water.
- Height 2′–3′.
- Trichome rate 7, Density rate 9.

Image 5.17

Tibouchina urvilleana, Princess Flower.

Image 5.18 *Gynura aurantiaca*, Velvet Plant.

- Grows in zones 9–12.
- Plant leaves have deep green and purple coloration.
- Adds texture to plant groupings.
- Plant used as a speciwomxn or as part of a group of potted plants.
- Can grow in high to medium light with medium water.
- Height 1′–2′, spread 2′–4′.
- Trichome rate 9, Density rate 8.

Image 5.18

Gynura aurantiaca, Velvet Plant.

Image 5.19 *Plectranthus* "Mona Lavender," Mona Lavender.

- Grows in zones 10–11.
- Has a full growth habit that fills a space.
- Plant has delicate purple flowers.
- Plant used for adding beauty to any room.
- Grows best in high indirect light with medium water.
- Height 1′–2′, spread 1′–2′.
- Trichome rate 7, Density rate 10.

Image 5.19

Plectranthus "Mona Lavender," Mona Lavender.

Image 5.20 *Sinningia cardinalis*, Cardinal Flower.

Grows in zone 11.
Has beautiful tubular orange/red flowers.
Plant has great texture and coloring.
Plant looks great potted in any room of the house.
Grows best in indirect light with medium water.
Height 1′–2′, spread 1′–2′.
Trichome rate 8, Density rate 7.

Image 5.20

Sinningia cardinalis, Cardinal Flower.

Image 5.21 *Achimenes* Hybrids, Hot Water Plant.

Grows in zones 7–8.
Has beautiful flowers that come in many different colors depending on the variety.
Plant adds a pop of color to any room.
Plant used for pots on tables or the floor.
Can grow in high indirect light with medium water and humidity.
Height 12″–24″, spread 3″–6″.
Trichome rate 8, Density rate 8.

Image 5.21

Achimenes Hybrids, Hot Water Plant.

Image 5.22 *Mikania ternate*, Plush Vine.

Grows in zone 10.
Leaves are green with a beautiful purple haze.
Plant has a fantastic texture and a glorious messy look.
Looks great in a hanging basket.
Can grow in bright indirect light.
Has medium water and humidity requirements.
Height 8″–12″, spread 18″–24″.
Trichome rate 8, Density rate 10.

Image 5.22

Mikania ternate, Plush Vine.

Image 5.23 *Swainsona formosa*, Glory Pea.

Grows in zones 9–11.
Has interestingly unique red flowers.
Plant adds a conversation piece to a room.
Plant grows best in high light with medium water.
Prefers dry air.
Can be difficult to grow outside of the native habitat.
Height 6″–12″, spread 12″–24″.
Trichome rate 8, Density rate 8.

Image 5.23

Swainsona formosa, Glory Pea.

Image 5.24 *Mammillaria hahniana*, Old Lady Cactus.

Grows in zones 9–11.
Has delicate pink flowers when in bloom.
Plant is perfect for a table top planter.
Grows best with high light and low water.
Height 10″, spread 20″.
Trichome rate 10, Density rate 10.

Image 5.24

Mammillaria hahniana, Old Lady Cactus.

Image 5.25 *Cyanotis kewensis*, Teddy Bear Vine.

Grows in zones 10–11.
Has soft fuzzy leaves that are uniquely mossy in color.
Looks great in hanging baskets.
Plant grows well in high to medium light, as well as under fluorescent lights.
Plant has medium water requirements.
Plant pictured is a related variety but looks very similar.
Height 6″–8″, spread 12″–24″.
Trichome rate 9, Density rate 10.

Image 5.25

Cyanotis kewensis, Teddy Bear Vine.

Image 5.26 *Cyanotis somaliensis*, Kitten Ears.

Grows in zones 10–11.
Has great texture with its fuzzy leaves.
Plant looks great in a hanging basket.
Grows best in high to medium light.
Plant likes low water and high humidity.
Height 6", spread 18".
Trichome rate 9, Density rate 9.

Image 5.26

Cyanotis somaliensis, Kitten Ears.

GREEN DESIGN SUMMARY

Using a mixture of plants is beneficial for design. For this site, this means using a combination of plants which have a high transpiration rate, plant hairs or trichomes on leaves, plants which grow with a thick density of leaves, as well as plants which produce oxygen at night, have pleasing scents, grow with the light conditions of the site, and plants and designs which change over time with magical moments during the process.

The redesign of this home requires a space which is above 70°F, above 43% humidity, has lots of natural sunlight, and multiple people using the space – all of which creates an atmosphere for stomata to open. The combination of these factors is beneficial for the health of the people in the home.

Image 5.27

Vertical garden in a home.

Image 5.28

Modern interior with hanging glass jars with air plants.

Images 5.27 through 5.29 illustrate some unique living green designs which have been applied in rooms. Existing structures for plants for homes, offices, restaurants, and more can be purchased, or unique site-specific designs can be built. Vertical garden kits for interior and exterior sites are available from multiple manufacturers. The aesthetic of

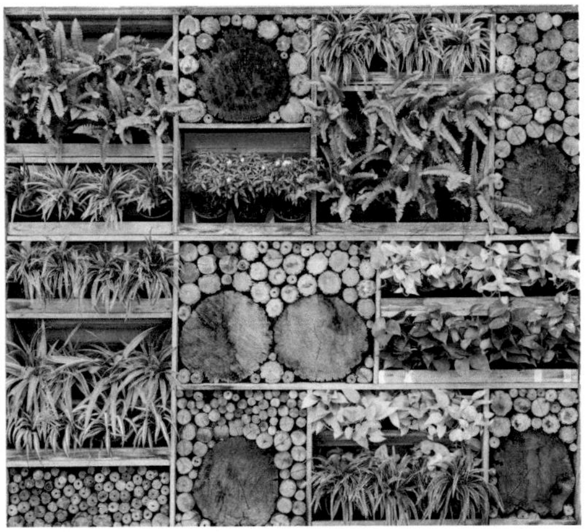

Image 5.29

Modern vertical design with living plants.

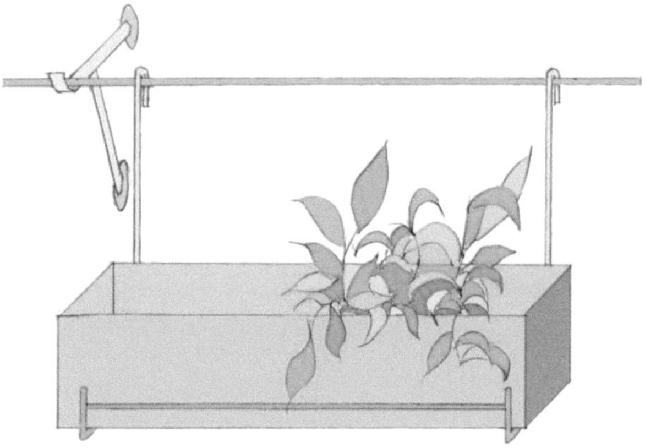

Image 5.30

Wall planters are designed gallery style. A supported bar allows planters to be hung at varying heights.

plants choices as well as shapes, depth, materials, lights, and more can be customized for each site to improve the plant growth.

The living green design for this home looks at each room as its own separate area rather than as a connected design. The living room has a visual connection to the kitchen and dining room and therefore some similar materials in the pots and plants are used to connect the spaces to feel as if the first floor is a garden which has multiple planted rooms. The plants weave into the lights and through the space in natural unexpected beautiful ways and through time create moments of daily change.

The rooms on the top floor have doors which close and therefore do not need to feel connected. Having separate rooms is important for the members of a family for privacy. Creating separate gardens for each room which push the boundary between garden and bedroom – or garden and office – is a design choice. There is a difference between merely a functional design which reduces the flu infectiousness versus a design which feels soothing and healing to be in.

There are multiple ways to design while applying the functions of the *Famulari Theory* to a site. This home and the other green designs in this book go beyond function to a form or aesthetic which pushes the balance of a room or site as living gardens, growing green spaces, magical living forms which change, grow, and heal the soul of the people and the health of the environment.

REFERENCES

Famulari, S. (2020). *Green Up! Sustainable Design Solutions for Healthier Work and Living Environments.* New York: Productivity Press. doi:10.4324/9780429297434

Chapter 6

Exterior Urban Rooftop in Residential Building, New York City

Image 6.1

The rooftop garden is primarily for spring through autumn use with materials that work in wind and direct sun.

DOI: 10.4324/9781003136880-7

EXISTING SITE INFORMATION

The 15th story rooftop has a gathering space for the shareholders with a kitchenette, restroom, tables, chairs, a shade structure, planters and views of downtown, midtown, the East River and Brooklyn Bridge, and the Hudson River and New Jersey. The gathering space on the roof is used by the tenants of the building all year round with 24-hour access in New York City. The primary seasons of use are spring through autumn. The plants selected are primarily for these seasons, with some structural plants for winter interest, particularly for holding snow on the plant for a sculptural shape and contrast of white snow to the dark plant structure.

The space is approximately 860 square feet. On rooftop designs, dead weight and live weight are important to address. The dead weight includes the weight of the roof itself as well as all permanent structures which are attached to the roof (the tiles, shade structure, kitchenette appliances, planters, soil, etc.). The live load includes any temporary or moving objects (the moving tables, people, snow, etc.). There are also snow load weights. These weights are based on the structure, and an engineer determines the load-bearing capacity of the roof.

Image 6.2

Urban rooftop in New York City. The 15th story rooftop has a gathering space for the shareholders with a kitchenette, restroom, tables, chairs, a shade structure, planters, and views of downtown, midtown, the East River and Brooklyn Bridge, and the Hudson River and New Jersey.

Image 6.3

Urban rooftop in New York City. Entry to the roof with tall grasses in planters.

Image 6.4

Urban rooftop in New York City with seating, shade structures and planters.

Image 6.5

Urban rooftop in New York City. Seating for multiple people to gather in the shade or sun allows for a variety of arrangements of seating options.

Image 6.6

Urban rooftop in New York City. Smaller tables are weighted for the wind on the roof, though they can be moved around.

The planters are approximately 3′ in height, with 6″ of stones on the bottom of each for drainage, and engineered soil – a soil which is lighter in weight, to help keep the dead weight well within the range of the requirements.

The tiles are raised above the roofline on short risers. The space between the tiles and roof is where rainwater drains to, irrigation and electric pipes are placed, and other infrastructure is hidden from view. The tiles can be lifted for repairs or changes.

The US plant zone is 7b, and there are plants which grow in the warm seasons and live through the winter seasons.

The access, walkways and gathering spaces are ADA complaint in width and slope to allow room for those with walking impairments.

Rooftops typically have to be designed to address windy conditions; because when on a roof, the effects of gentle to strong winds are amplified because there are no barriers which block or redirect wind. Structures are bolted down, selected outdoor furniture is typically heavier, and plants must be able to endure wind.

Image 6.7

Urban rooftop in New York City. The view to the cityscape is framed in the front with a variety of plants.

The irrigation is used from spring through autumn, set on timer for the seasons. During the winter the water is flushed from the system and turned off. Rainwater is not the primary source of water for the roof, though rainwater does supplement the existing irrigation in planters which are exposed to the rain.

There are electric sources within the kitchenette, restroom, and designed into the beams of the shade structure and planters. Electricity is required for the irrigation to run as well as for lights for night use and kitchen use. The electric sources are designed into the infrastructure and permanent structures. As the roof is in full sunlight, lighting is primarily used for night enjoyment with lights on the beams under the shade structure as well as along the walls outside the entry doors and restrooms.

Image 6.8

Planters in this design need some mobility to allow for flexibility in moving the furniture around. The garden is enjoyable for the users while allowing views of the cityscape.

GREEN DESIGN SOLUTION

Multiple plants and other design approaches are used in the alteration of the rooftop to reduce the spread of the infectiousness of the airborne flu virus for users of the spaces as well as to create a space for mental enjoyment by being around plants and enjoying stunning views. These include:

- Adding diverse vines, including hanging vines, to the shade structure over the table
- Adding small planters on the table
- Adding tall grasses in planters around the edges of the rooftop to reduce the infectiousness of the airborne flu virus
- Adding moveable planters near seating to reduce the infectiousness of the airborne flu virus
- The addition of plants for reducing the soundwaves through the open rooftop
- Planting on the edge fencing with planters which are attached to either the metal edging or are placed on the ground
- Creating trellis structures for climbing plants to grow on the wall surface

Image 6.9

Planters on each of the tables have seasonal plants, while larger planters have plants which can grow for multiple years, can move with the wind for visual appeal, and are most effective for the *Famulari Theory* during the warmer seasons.

Humidity and temperature are determined by outside weather conditions more than the plants themselves. Though sub-climates can be made in outdoor designs through the use of plants and walls, the subtle difference for a space such as this is not notable. Therefore, plants which grow in zone 7b are selected for this design.

Outdoor spaces, particularly rooftops, have a natural movement through the wind. Additionally, rooftops are windier than street level. This design reduces some of the wind for the user's enjoyment, as well as celebrating it with tall grasses and other plants which sway in the wind.

Finally, engineered soil is used to reduce the weight of the materials on the roof. Rooftops have load-bearing weights which are determined by the structure. Reducing the weight of stationary materials such as planters and large tables helps to allow space and weight for more huwomxns to enjoy the space.

Plants on the main table and above the main large table provide shade, color, scent, and an overhead plane of plants to help create a sub-space which can reduce the airborne virus. To protect the plants on the table from moving with the wind, the table has holes in the surface

Image 6.10

The table has an area designed for pots to sit below the table height, hiding the pots to better reveal the leaves and flowers. Vines grow throughout the shade structure.

which are designed for specific sized plants. These plants are taken indoors and cared for over the colder season or changed annually.

With wind naturally moving an airborne virus across the space, plants with clumps of leaf surfaces, plants with trichomes (plant hairs), plants which have a rough or sticky surface, and plants which have a high transpiration rate are beneficial to the site design. The taller structures with plants serve to reduce the effects of the wind while also filtering the air through the plants.

The design of the garden of plants on the roof is a colorful foreground to the background of the urban landscape. Views of the urban landscape are stunning and a daily experience for people to enjoy. Creating a rooftop design with the *Famulari Theory* for the reduction of the airborne flu virus also considers views, sounds, use of the space, urban air contaminants, wind, and other site-specific needs.

Where there is seating there are planters within a few feet. The planters may be permanent or moveable, and are within seating arrangements, even when re-arrangements are made. The plants frame views without blocking them as views can be seen in both the immediate distance as well as the longer views of sites.

Image 6.11

The rooftop garden has planters above the restroom as well as throughout the space to create a garden for enjoyment as well as improved health.

Tall grasses are used for multiple purposes in both the reduction of the airborne flu virus as well as a design feature to celebrate the wind. With the grasses growing as much as 3 feet tall above the planters, the grasses do not block the views from a roof. The tufts of the top of the grasses are not only colorful and make a subtle sound in the wind; they also have fuzzy tufts which are beneficial for designing with the *Famulari Theory*.

Colorful plantings are part of the design aesthetic for the rooftop. The plants have diverse textures, shapes, and heights. The kaleidoscope of colorful plants helps to create a design which explores the edges of an urban garden and rooftop.

Rooftop designs use rainwater and building water in the irrigation. Irrigation is part of the infrastructure of a rooftop design, with water containers for rainwater as well as additional water for irrigation, sinks, and restrooms. The pipes and tubing are below the pavers for areas which need water. Though moveable planters may be rolled anywhere on the rooftop, it is beneficial to create some areas where water sources are readily available to be easily able to connect to the moving planters. In this way, when the planters are moved to certain areas, they can be connected to irrigation which is below the pavers.

Image 6.12

This rooftop has structures covered in plants as well as plants of varying sizes, textures, colors, and blooming times during the year.

The larger planter at the entry to the roof is planted with diverse plantings including some plants with densely clumping leaves, some with trichomes, some with high transpiration rates, and some which remove urban air contaminants. With larger areas for planting, an overhead shade structure, and a series of moveable and non-moveable planters, the totality of the plants creates the spatial design.

The design in this chapter allows for the combination of rooftop and garden with structures of the site still being notably visible. The design can be shifted to have even more plants, including plants which cover structures with more color, textures, and opportunities for daily growth and change in the design. Image 6.12 illustrates this point with rooftop design which covers structures with the colors and textures of plants which change year round.

PLANTS IN THE SITE DESIGN

Plants for the rooftop are chosen based on the plant zone, ability to grow in windy conditions, ability to grow in shallow planters, transpiration rate of the plant, and growth pattern of the leaves – including those that grow with more densely packed leaves, and plants with trichomes.

The plant zone for this rooftop design in downtown Manhattan is 7b. Plants which grow in that plant zone or colder (zones 1–6) can be used.

In addition to the functional needs for designing a space which reduces the infectiousness of the airborne flu virus, plants are also chosen to enhance the rooftop space and make it feel welcoming, healthy, and enjoyable for the users of the rooftop to enjoy the views and move some of the furniture around for events in the space. There is an aesthetic balance between an engaging green urban rooftop which frames views of the city with healthy plants and merely placing planters in a space. Balancing it all is one of the reasons for the design choices.

Information on plant selections for this site is included, as well as trichome and density rates. Plants are listed from largest in scale to smaller. In Chapter 9 there is further information about the plant trichome and density rates. Further information on these plants and others can be found at www.steviefamulari.net/Famulari-Theory.

Image 6.13 *Muhlenbergia capillaris*, Muhly Grass.

Grows in zones 5–11.
Has four-season interest.
Plant has movement in the wind and great texture.
Plant used for screening, wind break, or as a speciwomxn plant.
Can grow in sun and partial shade, drought, and wind.
Height 3′, spread 3′.
Trichome rate 10, Density rate 8.

Image 6.13

Muhlenbergia capillaris, Muhly Grass.

Image 6.14 *Lavandula stoechas*, Spanish Lavender.

Grows in zones 7–10.
Has spring through summer interest.
Plant has a great scent, bloom color, and attracts pollinators.
Plant used for containers and beds.
Can grow in sun, heat, and drought.
Height 24″–30″, spread 24″–30″.
Trichome rate 7, Density rate 10.

Image 6.14

Lavandula stoechas, Spanish Lavender.

Image 6.15 *Helianthus argophyllus*, Silverleaf Sunflower.

Grows in zones 2–11.
Has summer to fall interest.
Plant adds a burst of color and height, and attracts pollinators.
Can grow in sun and drought.
Plant is low maintenance.
Height 4′–6′, spread 1′–2′.
Trichome rate 9, Density rate 7.

Image 6.15

Helianthus argophyllus, Silverleaf Sunflower.

Image 6.16 *Artemisia* "Powis Castle," Powis Castle Artemisia.

Grows in zones 4–9.
Has four-season interest.
Plant has texture and fragrance.
Used for complementing grasses and container planting.
Can grow in sun and drought.
Height 30″, spread 36″.
Trichome rate 7, Density rate 10.

Image 6.16

Artemisia "Powis Castle," Powis Castle Artemisia.

Image 6.17 *Artemisia stelleriana* "Silver Brocade," Dusty Miller.

- Grows in zones 5–10.
- Has four-season interest.
- Plant has a scent and fantastic fuzzy texture.
- Works great in containers.
- Can grow in sun, drought, humidity, and freezing temperatures.
- Height 12", spread 29".
- Trichome rate 9, Density rate 9.

Image 6.17

Artemisia stelleriana "Silver Brocade," Dusty Miller.

Image 6.18 *Hedera helix*, English Ivy.

- Grows in zones 5–10.
- Has four-season interest.
- Plant has vertical appeal and durability.
- Can be grown on trellises and green walls.
- Easily grows in varying light and water conditions.
- Height 20'–80', spread 3'–50'.
- Trichome rate 1, Density rate 9.

Image 6.18

Hedera helix, English Ivy.

Image 6.19 *Teucrium polium*, Felty Germander.

- Grows in zones 6–9.
- Has summer to fall interest.
- Plant used as a ground cover and for vertical coverage.
- Can grow in full sun and drought.
- Plant produces yellow flowers in July in zone 7.
- Height 4"–16", spread 6"–12".
- Trichome rate 8, Density rate 8.

Image 6.19

Teucrium polium, Felty Germander.

GREEN DESIGN SUMMARY

Rooftop designs can be as creative as the people involved, ranging from wildflower fields to trees, as well as agriculture to urban forests. Some plants which are effective for the *Famulari Theory* are available at www.StevieFamulari.net/Famulari-Theory, and must be reviewed for plants that will work for a specific site.

There is a balance in designing a rooftop to create a design in which people can enjoy views while also having living plants, seating, irrigation, permanent elements, and moveable elements, while all working effectively with the load-bearing weight of the roof.

Image 6.20

Rooftop garden in Singapore.

Image 6.21

Green roof in Fukuoka, Japan.

Image 6.22

Bosco Verticale skyscraper (vertical forest) in Milan, Italy.

There are multiple design choices to consider beyond function, such as "what does the space feel like," or "how does it make the user feel." This living green rooftop explores the design question – is this rooftop a garden, or is it a space for people to gather? This creative rooftop design can help people to explore both.

Chapter 7

Exterior Urban Courtyard of Residential Building in Bronx, NY

Image 7.1

Courtyard garden with extensive plantings for full year use.

DOI: 10.4324/9781003136880-8

EXISTING SITE INFORMATION

Urban Courtyard for Residential Building in the South Bronx, NY

The courtyard is designed within the 6-story building of 149 apartments and contains a gated entry from the street. One entry has steps, while the other one has a ramp for wheelchair access.

Image 7.2

Courtyard in Bronx, NY. The courtyard has 2 entry gates, one with a ramp for ADA design.

Image 7.3

Courtyard in Bronx, NY. The edges of the courtyard are planted with a row of small trees and shrubs.

Image 7.4

Courtyard in Bronx, NY. The planters are shallow with small plants.

The courtyard with a planted edge is approximately 3,150 square feet and is used by the tenants and shareholders of the building all year round and throughout the day and night. The street lights, building entry lights, and lights from the apartment windows shed enough light for use of the courtyard at night for relaxing and meeting friends. An urban space of this size can hold multiple people at one time.

There is one bench which can comfortably seat two people and seven planters in the space. The space is used for relaxing, as well as for events when folding tables and chairs are brought to use.

The plant zone is 7b. The plant zone is based on the temperature range and is used to help determine which plants can grow in the area.

Many of the center-row plants are in shallow planters of 3′ deep, while the edge plants and the Japanese dwarf maple tree in the center are in shallow ground soil. The soil

Image 7.5

Courtyard in Bronx, NY. The front entry is not symmetrical, and has the opportunity to celebrate a balanced non-symmetrical design with more diverse plantings.

continues below the pavers for both the edge plantings and the Japanese dwarf maple planting. The edge plants are behind a fence. There is water access in the courtyard with a hose used for watering all the plants. There are also electrical outlets in the courtyard.

The urban sounds of the area in the South Bronx are typical, with cars, people walking and talking, children playing in the courtyard, in the winter creating snow designs, and using the space to read a book. Across the street from the courtyard is a park.

At one gate there are three steps from the street level into the courtyard. At the other gate there is a ramp which is compliant with the American with Disabilities Act (ADA) in width and slope to allow room for those with a walking impairment and those who require a wheelchair. The entry to the building also has a small ramp for use with ADA design.

The courtyard has approximately a 1% slope across the site, with water draining from the street to the front of the building, and angled to drain into the edge plantings. This slope is barely noticeable by people and primarily serves for water drainage, though it also is part of the natural terrain of this area in the Bronx.

The tenants of the building overlook the courtyard. The tenants and owners of the apartments on the lower floors use plants in the courtyard, plants inside the house, and blinds in their windows for semi-privacy from others seeing their apartments. Full privacy is not typically part of the urban experience, something which many urbanites accept as part of the urban lifestyle. Plants, both exterior and interior, can serve to provide semi-privacy in an urban fashion.

Image 7.6

Courtyard in Bronx, NY. The ADA ramp entry to the courtyard allows access to the space for those requiring a ramp for walking mobility.

Image 7.7

As a green design solution the courtyard garden has permeable pavers with plants between the pavers, planters on wheels, and vertical plants weaving throughout the building surface and entry gates.

GREEN DESIGN SOLUTION

Multiple plants and other design approaches are used in the alteration of the courtyard to reduce the spread of the infectiousness of the airborne flu virus for users of the spaces as well as to improve the overall air quality and psychological benefits of being around plants. These include:

- Removing the gates which act as a cage for the plants to allow more space for plants to grow in the courtyard which assists to reduce the infectiousness of the airborne flu virus
- Adding additional seating and a table for a gathering of the shareholders and tenants of the building
- Using only one entry and creating a larger green space in the courtyard for plants
- Adding planter boxes to all windows throughout the building
- Adding decorative structures for the plants in the window planter boxes to grow
- Creating trellis structures for vines to grow in front of the building and not on the building structure itself
- Plantings on the small roof above the front door

Image 7.8

The trees and plants create an urban green space for the urban dwellers as well as semi-privacy for the people on the lower floors of the building through a variety of plants.

- Adding plants near seating to reduce the infectiousness of the airborne flu virus
- Using the sidewalk gate structure as an area for plant design
- The addition of plants for reducing the soundwaves through the open courtyard
- Creating an outdoor courtyard as a pleasant easy space for people to gather, inspiring people to be outdoors rather than indoors. Outdoor warm spaces have more air circulation to help reduce the spread of the airborne flu virus

Humidity and temperature are determined by outside weather conditions more than the plants themselves. Though sub-climates can be made in courtyards through the use of plants and walls, the subtle difference for a space such as this is not notable. Therefore, plants which grow in zone 7b are selected for this design.

Above the entry to the building the small rooftop is used for plants which grow through the edge and over the top.

Planters are added near the door entry and window lobby to create a sense of entry or exit into the garden. The sense of entry is not only visually appealing but also appealing with the wind rustling through the plants and scent moving through the breeze.

The primary seasons for users of this courtyard are spring through autumn. The time period in New York City when the temperature and humidity are most effective for the *Famulari Theory* to work best is late spring through autumn.

The ADA entry can be the sole entry for the courtyard while closing the other entry and using the space to add plant materials and seating for the shareholders.

Planters which are placed near where people are sitting are specifically selected for their density of leaves and trichomes to address reducing flu infectiousness. Creating conditions with light, humidity, *and people naturally* breathing out carbon dioxide boosts the stomata to open, adding further transpiration and an area for holding air contaminants.

> Plants can absorb sound through their leaves and foliage. Dense trees are more effective than trees in large spaces without greenery. The bark of trees is a hard surface which sound waves bounce off and scatter. The green areas of plants are soft and have pockets of air. When sound waves are directed to the foliage, the sound waves are softened and absorbed into the leaves and air pockets, similar to a soft sponge. This is effective for urban areas where there are many sounds which move through the air.
>
> **(Famulari, 2020)**

> When dense areas of plant materials are in front of buildings, properties, courtyards, yards, entrances, or windows, the plants act as sponges for sound waves. These plantings reduce the sound that travels to residents in the building, property, courtyard, yard, or room.
>
> **(Famulari, 2020)**

The same effects work for indoor plants as well as outdoor plants.

Image 7.9

The courtyard garden has seating for multiple people to gather as well as plants which grow at the ground plane, seating height, standing height, and above huwomxn height. The full scope of plants is needed for an effective garden design with the *Famulari Theory.*

Image 7.10

Adding gardens above the entry as well as on all windows adds to the total green space, both horizontally and vertically. The totality of the green space is expanded, improving the air quality and the health of the people in the space.

The diverse plants in this courtyard design are selected for reducing the infectiousness of the airborne flu virus as well as for sound absorption, improved ecological system, seasonal interest, and creating a green space which improves air quality, privacy for residents on lower floors, and shareholder enjoyment.

Adding to the green space, all windows have shallow planters on the outside of the building. The planters have diverse plantings which may include artful structures for plants to grow vertically. The plants are colorful, have a variety of textures and growing shapes, and add to the overall green space. These plants are not selected specifically for the qualities needed in the *Famulari Theory*. With over 150 windows facing this courtyard, the quantity of plants added to the building front helps to improve the overall air quality and create an atmosphere of an urban green space.

Small trees may be planted into the ground with the removal of the concrete slabs. The courtyard ground surface is changed to permeable pavers, allowing water to drain through the pavers and plants to grow in parts of the ground. There are multiple different types of patterns for permeable pavers, some with more and less space for water to drain and plants to grow. Water for plants is through a hose connected to the building.

Some plants are placed in large planters which are designed to stay in one location long term. Planter gardens are a valuable alternative when the ground surface is not available to plant. Large planters in this design are for long-term growth, with the planter being chosen based on the mature scale of the plant. Smaller planters can be moved with care indoors to the lobby during the colder seasons.

Image 7.11

Permeable pavers allow water to run through spaces and plants to grow between the patterned stones. There are a variety of styles and patterns of permeable pavers which have varying amounts of plants growing in the design.

Plants are designed for placement on the ground level, the eye level, and the overhead plane (about huwomxn height). Taller plants create canopies of shade, dancing shadows in the wind, and semi-privacy for shareholders in the lower floors. With plants on these three height ranges, the *Famulari Theory* can be most effective in reducing the airborne flu virus, as well as creating a space for improving urban air quality and creating a space with reduced street sounds and increase mental enjoyment.

Similar to plazas where a single huwomxn or a group of people come to enjoy the space, the company of people, or to celebrate the magic of the day – this courtyard has many moments of change for people to enjoy throughout all seasons. Plants have the lovely ability to show time, growth, and change in both short-term blooms and the long-term scale of trees. The plants in this courtyard allow moments of magic when a bloom appears, a scent passes through the air, and colors change. The ability to have the magic of a green courtyard, while also selecting plants for reducing the airborne flu virus, and improving urban air quality and creating spaces for people to enjoy with growing plants – it is the beauty and wonder of effective green design.

PLANTS IN THE SITE DESIGN

Plants for the courtyard redesign are chosen based on the plant zone, the transpiration rate of the plant, and the growth pattern of the leaves – including those that grow with more densely packed leaves, and plants with trichomes. The plant zone for this courtyard in the Bronx, NY, is 7b. Plants which grow in that plant zone or colder (zones 1–6) can be used.

In addition to the functional needs for designing a space which reduces the infectiousness of the airborne flu virus, plants are also chosen to enhance the courtyard space and make it feel welcoming, healthy, and enjoyable to the shareholders through color, scent, textures, sound from moving wind, and the growing structure of the plant as it reaches full maturity. There is an aesthetic balance between an engaging green urban design and merely plants in a space. Balancing it all is one of the reasons for the design choices.

Information on plant selections for this site is included, as well as trichome and density rates. Plants are listed from largest in scale to smallest. In Chapter 9 there is further information about the plant trichome and density rates. Further information on these plants and others can be found at www.steviefamulari.net/Famulari-Theory.

Image 7.12 *Cotinus coggygria*, Smoke Tree.

Grows in zones 4–11.
Has three-season interest.
Plant has great texture and bright fall color.
Can be used to reduce noise and is an interesting speciwomxn piece.
Can grow in sun and various soil types.
Height 10′–15′, spread 10′–15′.
Trichome rate 6, Density rate 10.

Image 7.12

Cotinus coggygria, Smoke Tree.

Image 7.13 *Cotoneaster franchetii*, Franchet Cotoneaster.

Grows in zones 6–9.
Has four-season interest.
Plant is a dense shrub with an appealing growth habit and attractive fall fruit.
Used as a screen, wind break, or as a speciwomxn plant.
Can grow in sun, drought, poor soil, and is salt tolerant.
Height 6′–10′, spread 4′–8′.
Trichome rate 7, Density rate 10.

Image 7.13

Cotoneaster franchetii, Franchet Cotoneaster.

Image 7.14 *Verbascum thapsus*, Great Mullein.

Grows in zones 3–9.
Has summer to fall interest.
Plant has great texture and bright yellow flowers.
Plant used as a specimen with interesting shape and texture.
Can grow in sun, drought, and dry soil.
Height 7′, spread 2.5′.
Trichome rate 10, Density rate 9.

Image 7.14

Verbascum thapsus, Great Mullein.

Image 7.15 *Cortaderia selloana* "Pumila," Dwarf Pampas Grass.

Grows in zones 6–10.
Has late summer through winter interest.
Plant has movement in the wind and texture.
Plant used for screening, wind break or as a speci-womxn plant.
Can grow in sun and light shade, drought, wind.
Height 36″–72″, spread 36″–48″.
Trichome rate 7, Density rate 9.

Image 7.15

Cortaderia selloana "Pumila," Dwarf Pampas Grass.

Image 7.16 *Helianthus mollis*, Ashy Sunflower.

Grows in zones 4–9.
Has summer through fall interest.
Plant has fabulous flowers and attracts pollinators.
Plant used for adding color and height to beds and containers.
Can grow in sun and light shade, drought, dry soil.
Height 2′–4′, spread 1′–3′.
Trichome rate 7, Density rate 7.

Image 7.16

Helianthus mollis, Ashy Sunflower.

Image 7.17 *Papaver rhoeas*, Common Poppy.

Grows in zones 3–10.
Has late spring to early summer interest.
Plant has fantastic red flowers.
Plant used for adding a bright accent color to beds and containers.
Can grow in full sun and is low maintenance.
Height 9″–18″, spread 6″–12″.
Trichome rate 7, Density rate 7.

Image 7.17

Papaver rhoeas, Common Poppy.

Image 7.18 *Oxalis adenophylla*, Silver Shamrock.

Grows in zones 3–9.
Has late spring to early summer interest.
Plant has interesting foliage and pretty flowers.
Its petite size makes it perfect for small planters.
Can grow in sun, light shade, and various soil types.
Height 4″, spread 6″.
Trichome rate 7, Density rate 10.

Image 7.18

Oxalis adenophylla, Silver Shamrock.

GREEN DESIGN SUMMARY

Urban design can have unique green solutions when creative designers and communities are involved in the dialogue and design. Using the vertical spaces along with rainwater is beneficial to urban greening. With the great variety of plants and planting spaces in urban spaces, greening can be used to improve the overall health of the people and urban environment.

For example, if all or most windows across a building have planted window boxes, this alone would be a sight of amazement for people to enjoy throughout the seasons and can improve health and the environment.

Image 7.19

Metal fence with plants growing through, irrigated with rainwater.

The design aesthetic of this courtyard is not merely to address the needed elements of the *Famulari Theory*. This courtyard is designed to push the boundaries of urban garden vs. urban courtyard. This aesthetic is shown not only in the quantity, scale, and variety of plants used but also in the spaces the plants are growing. This design breaks the straight connecting architectural lines of the space to have curves and broken amorphous shapes. A huwomxn is able to experience the site as an urban garden, an urban courtyard, or a unique combination of both.

Image 7.20

Planter boxes on a business building front.

Section 2

The *Famulari Theory*, Breaking Down the Theory

Chapter 8

The *Famulari Theory*, Breaking Down the Theory and the Influenza Virus

INTRODUCTION TO SECTION 2

This second section of *Designing Green Spaces for Health* explains the multiple elements of the *Famulari Theory* in further detail. There are many studies and research noted in the reference pages of this book for further resources on some of the specific items discussed here.

These chapters are easiest read in a step-by-step order to best explain each of the conditions of the *Famulari Theory*. The step-by-step order of the sections builds to the totality of the theory. During the breakdown of the different aspects of the theory, images relevant to the science, virus, study, plant, or other elements are used to help illustrate the points or other items discussed. How the different pieces of the theory relate to the totality of the *Famulari Theory* is described throughout this second section of the book, as well as in the closing chapter.

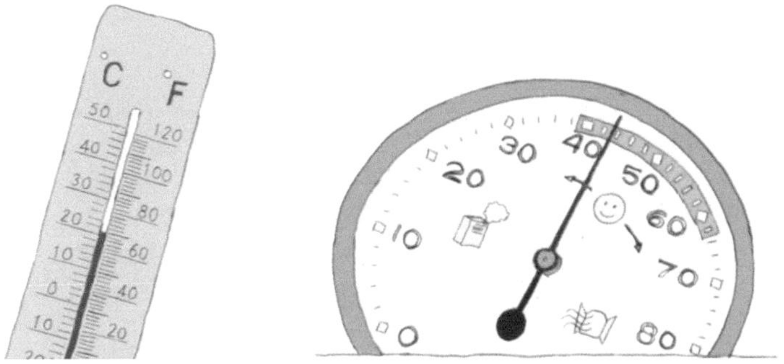

Image 8.1

The *Famulari Theory* has six pieces which reduce the infectiousness of airborne flu. In this chapter, the first piece of temperature and the fifth piece of humidity are explained in further detail. An understanding of the influenza (flu) virus is also explained in further detail.

DOI: 10.4324/9781003136880-10

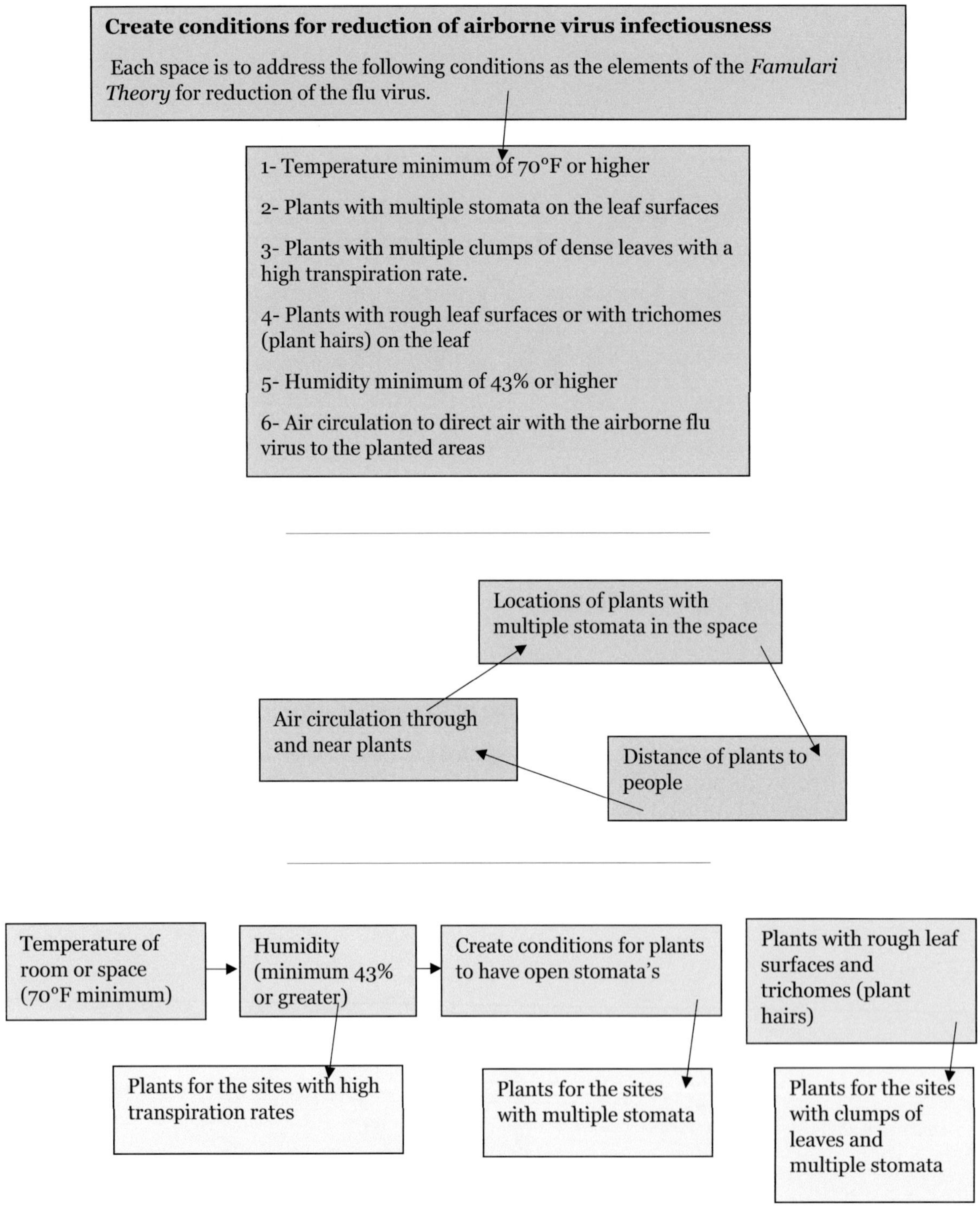

Image 8.2

Diagram of *Famulari Theory* elements.

The green research and sciences cross a range of fields – including phytoremediation, virology, horticulture, biology, earth sciences, chemistry, and other fields. It is the combination of them which captures the totality of the *Famulari Theory*.

This section of the book is the break down in further detail for continued dialogue. I recommend these chapters be read in order as some items build to the next item.

THE SIX PIECES OF THE *FAMULARI THEORY*

The chart (Image 8.2) is reintroduced to remind the reader of each of the pieces of the green theory, and how they relate to each other. A breakdown of the pieces, including background information, is included to more fully discuss the pieces.

GERMS, VIRUSES, AND MORE

Germs is a catch-all term that covers viruses, bacteria, and other microscopic particles. It is similar to using the term plants to cover trees, shrubs, annuals, perennials, succulents, and grasses. There are multiple types of germs or infectious agents. These include viruses, bacteria, fungi, protozoans, and helminths. A brief explanation of the term virus is offered in order to understand more about the structure.

Viruses

Viruses are smaller than bacteria, and even smaller than cells. Viruses cannot replicate without a host. A virus is not living, it is an object, not an organism. Though viruses contain RNA, viruses cannot self-replicate without a host (such as a plant, animal, or huwomxn).

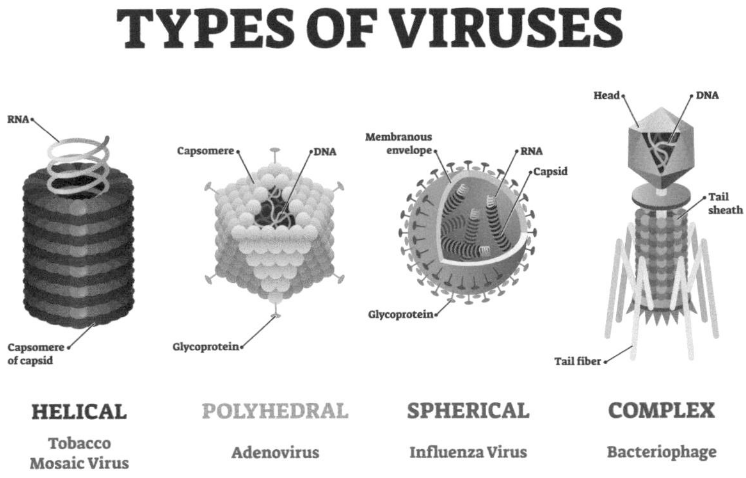

Image 8.3

Some examples of different virus structures.

Some commonly known viruses include AIDS, the common cold, Ebola, herpes, flu, measles, and chicken pox. Keeping one's body healthy (mentally and physically) helps to prime one's immune system to fight infections. People have multiple healthy ways of responding to viruses, some of which include coughing, mucus, drinking plenty of water, staying in higher humidity, and a build-up of antibodies to fight the virus.

The focus of this theory is specifically on viruses, and more specifically on the influenza or flu virus, due to its common occurrence, spread, scale, and availability of vaccines.

THE FLU VIRUS STRUCTURE

Explaining the influenza, or flu virus structure, starting in relatable terms to understand it is important. In its most basic form, a virus is a small structure which consists of genetic material (RNA in the case of the influenza virus, DNA for other viruses), surrounded by an envelope. RNA is at the genes of the influenza virus. Other viruses may have DNA, surround by a capsule coating or shell.

Viruses are not considered living. There are multiple definitions of life throughout herstory. Viruses do not meet the criteria of living in part because of its inability to respond to environmental changes, which is one characteristic of a living organism. A virus is also not self-sufficient, does not evolve, and needs a host to replicate. Therefore, since a virus is not living, it cannot die. Rather, viruses lose their infectiousness.

Viruses move around until their infectiousness is deteriorated or lost, or until they can attach themselves to a compatible cell of a host (i.e., plant, animal or huwomxn). Because each virus is specific to a host, viruses cannot replicate in different hosts. In other words – plant viruses cannot replicate in a person, and a huwomxn virus cannot replicate in a plant.

Once attached to a host cell, the virus enters the cell and releases its genetic material into the host's cell and tricks the host's cell machinery into replicating the virus genome RNA and building more virus particles. Then, the virus particles leave the cell and spread throughout the host and infect more host cells and/or move to other individual hosts. There are multiple mechanisms built into hosts (i.e., plants, animals, and huwomxns) to fight off viral infection.

Further Understanding of the Flu Virus Structure

In more specific terms, think of the flu virus as a sphere or small structure of genetic material (or genome), covered by an envelope and a capsid (coating). The envelope has a series of spikes (proteins) sticking to the surface of it. That same coating or envelope protects the interior structure (genome or genetic code) which has the RNA segments – the genetic material or genes of the virus. Image 8.4 is a labeled basic illustration of the flu virus.

The flu virus has a lipid envelope coating surrounding the genome or genetic code. The coating has two proteins shaped like spikes on its surface – hemagglutinin (HA or H) and neuraminidase (NA or N). Image 8.5 in this chapter illustrate these elements.

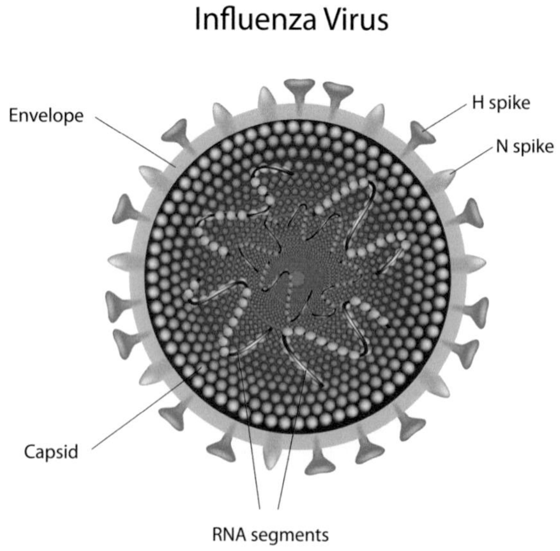

Image 8.4

Structure of the influenza virus.

When a new strand or flu subtype is found, it is named for the H and N proteins. For example, the 2009 flu outbreak was called H1N1[1] (McGill 2018), whereas the common seasonal flu is H3N2[1].

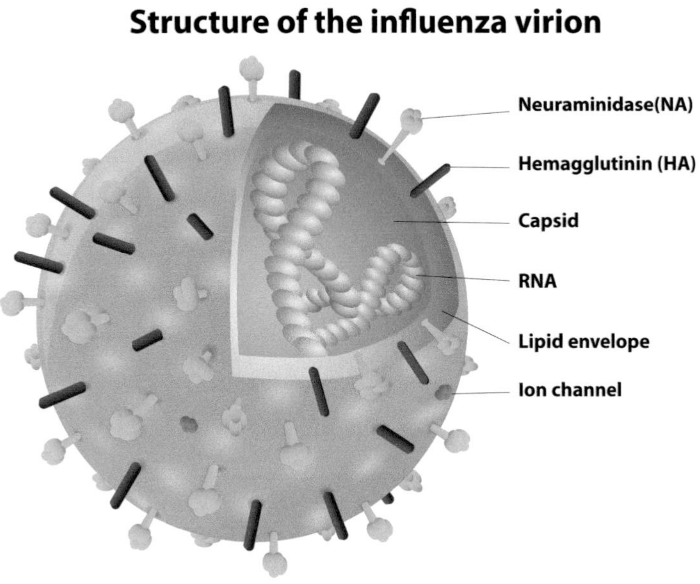

Image 8.5

Structure of the influenza virus.

Throughout this book I have made a point to state that viruses reduce or lose their infectiousness. This is because the flu virus is not living and therefore cannot die. Viruses are not living, whereas other germs are.

Therefore, the *Famulari Theory* looks at designing green spaces to reduce the airborne flu viruses through a series of design choices and interventions. There are a few ways to reduce the flu virus infectiousness or make it non-viable. These include higher temperatures, higher humidity, bleach, antibodies, sunlight, being out of a host for an extended time, filters, and more.

Size of Viruses

The size of the flu virus with the envelope is microscopic, that is, it cannot be seen without a microscope. It is measured in the unit of microns. A micron is equal to one-millionth of a meter. Hair is measured in microns, as are bacteria and viruses.

To understand the scale more clearly, Image 8.6 shows items in a range of scales, from large visible items to items which require a microscope to be seen. On the smaller scale, a huwomxn hair ranges from 30 microns to 100 microns – which is visible by the eye. Smoke ranges from 0.01 to 4 microns which requires a microscope to be seen. Smoke can be seen when there is a myriad of smoke particles together, as when you have burned some food while cooking and produced smoke. However, individual particles of smoke are too small to be seen without a microscope. Bacteria range from 0.3 to 5 microns, and smaller yet are viruses which generally range from 0.005 to 0.3 microns in size. Smoke, bacteria, and viruses require a microscope to see.

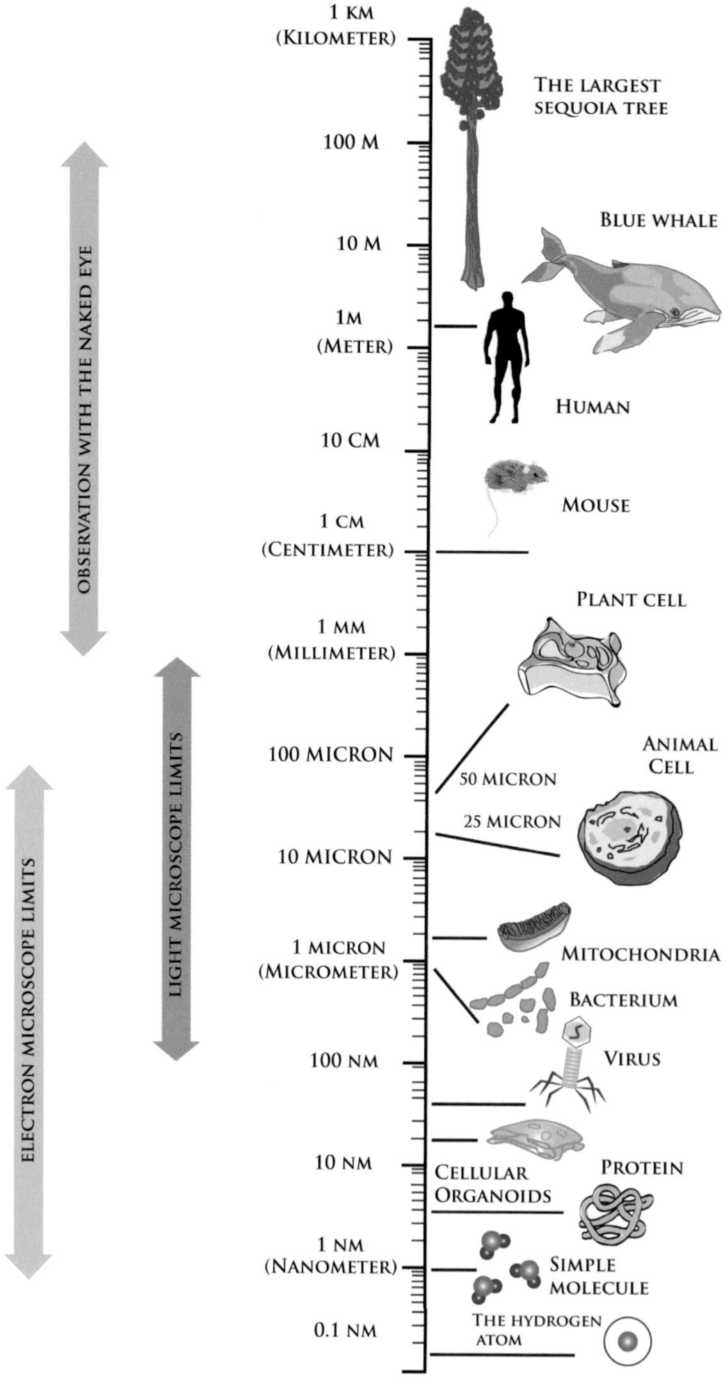

Image 8.6

Scale of some living elements visible to the eye through to microscopic scale.

DISTURBING THE DIFFERENT ELEMENTS OF THE FLU VIRUS STRUCTURE

The envelope of the flu virus has protein spikes on its surface. This pattern of protein spikes on the envelope of the virus is used to attach itself to a host cell, a huwomxn host. Without the envelope, the flu virus is not able to attach to a host cell.

In other words, the envelope around the virus' RNA is needed for the host in order to be recognized. The envelope can be removed before it reaches the host with cleaners and disinfectors. In removing the virus' envelope before it attaches to a host cell, the virus becomes non-infectious and is not able to attach to a host, and therefore will not infect the host.

"The virus envelope not only protects *the genome and core proteins but also* acts as a vector or route to transfer genome between host cells" (Greatorex 2010).

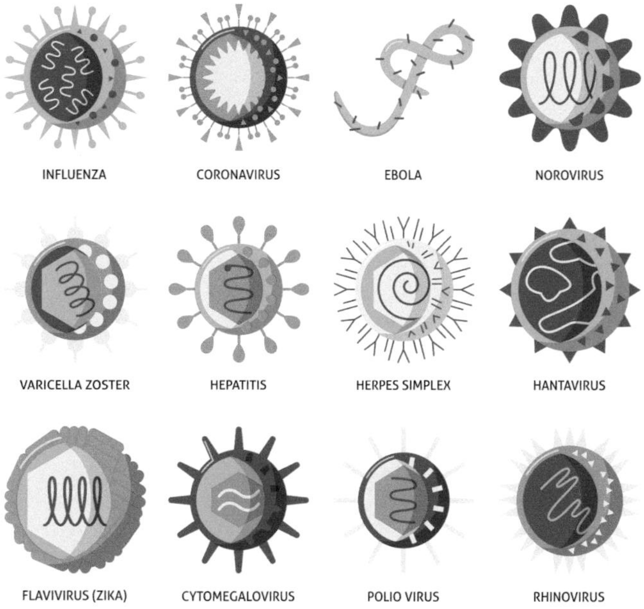

Image 8.7

Some examples of different virus structures.

Let me break that down a bit first to plain terms. The envelope with the spikes acts as the directional source which allows the virus to be transferred to a host cell. In other words, if a person who has the flu sneezes, the flu virus will be expelled into the air during the sneeze.

The droplets of liquid the person expels during a sneeze contains the flu virus with the protective envelope. That envelope acts as the track or directional source to attach to a host cell in a huwomxn. Once attached, the virus can transfer the RNA of the flu into the huwomxn cell and infect the host. Once the flu virus is inside the host and attaches to huwomxn cells, the envelope naturally disintegrates or is digested, thus allowing the virus RNA to infect the host.

"Disruption of the envelope either by lipid attack (causing disintegration) or protein denaturation (preventing fusion to host cells) inhibits the virus being transmitted to a new host" (Greatorex 2010).

In simpler terms, disturbing the envelope, by a few different sources or means (bleach, cleaners, heat, UV light) will disrupt the virus from being able to attach to a host. There are a few methods to disturb the envelope layer.

One method is a lipid attack. This is when the envelope is washed away by materials such as soap. This approach causes the envelope of the virus to disintegrate, therefore making it unable to attach to a host cell.

Another approach is protein denaturation. This is when proteins in the envelope and capsids are disintegrated by things such as bleach and heat. This approach disturbs protein function and prevents the fusion of the virus particles to a host cell.

Destruction of the protein (spikes on the envelopes) renders the virus non-infectious. With the spikes destroyed or altered, the virus does not have the ability to attach to a host cell. The protein spikes can be altered by cleaners, bleach, and heat.

Removal of the envelope while in the air or not attached to a viable host and exposing the genome makes the virus non-replicate-able.

Lastly, the center of the flu virus structure is where the RNA of the virus sits. This is what defines the virus as a flu virus, or any other virus. Destruction of the center of the flu virus structure, the genome, renders the virus non-infectious. This can be done by UV light or certain chemicals that target nucleic acids.

When a virus is unable to attach to a host for any of these reasons, it renders the virus non-viable. One additional note about the envelope of the virus. Once the flu virus is inside the host and attaches to huwomxn cells, the envelope naturally disintegrates or is digested, thus allowing the virus RNA to infect the host.

Flu Virus Replication in a Host and Why It Cannot Replicate in Plants

The flu virus requires a living host in order to replicate, and cannot replicate while in the air or landed on a surface. However, the flu virus can live on different surfaces and in different conditions for an extended time. An upcoming section "Airborne Flu Virus Infectiousness on Different Surfaces" specifically addresses the length of time the flu virus can stay infectious or viable on different surfaces.

Viruses and other contaminants can get into plants through available openings in the plants, though the flu virus will not infect the plant. In the case of the airborne flu virus, it may enter a plant through the leaves most notably (as opposed to roots, cuts in branches, broken branches, incorrect pruning, unhealed cut).

However, the flu virus can only replicate in the living host of a huwomxn or some closely related animal, as it is adapted to these hosts. Flu viruses cannot infect a plant.

This sentence is important to understand – the flu virus cannot replicate in plants, as plants do not have a cell structure which receives the huwomxn flu virus. Therefore, if an airborne flu virus from a sneeze finds its way to the surface of a plant, it will not replicate. The flu virus may sit on the plant leaf surface until, due to time and site conditions, it becomes non-viable or non-infectious.

In looking at the applications of this for the *Famulari Theory*, the airborne flu virus may arrive at the plant leaf which has open stomata (stomata are pore-like structures on the plant leaf; Chapter 9 explains more about plant stomata). Once on the plant leaf, the virus will be unable to move with air circulation for an extended time. Unable to move within the plant stomata or trichomes (plant hairs), the flu virus becomes non-viable and unable to infect a huwomxn.

WHAT COUGHS AND SNEEZES ARE MADE OF

A cough or sneeze forces air and liquid (mucus and saliva) from our bodies into the air. If a person has the flu virus in their body, their cough or sneeze contains the flu virus particles in the droplets of liquid which are expelled into the air during the sneeze. The flu virus is then airborne, moving through the air around the room or outdoor space.

There are approximately 16 ounces of liquid (½ liter/2.1 cups in the United States) in a person's lungs. That liquid can be expelled in coughs or sneezes (Lange, 1999). That is the equivalent of a water bottle of liquid. The liquid expelled in coughs contain over 3,000 droplets of fluid in each cough. This fluid contains the flu virus, which is then airborne.

Sneezes have more flu viruses, with over two hundred million (200,000,000) flu virus mircoorganisms contained in a sneeze.

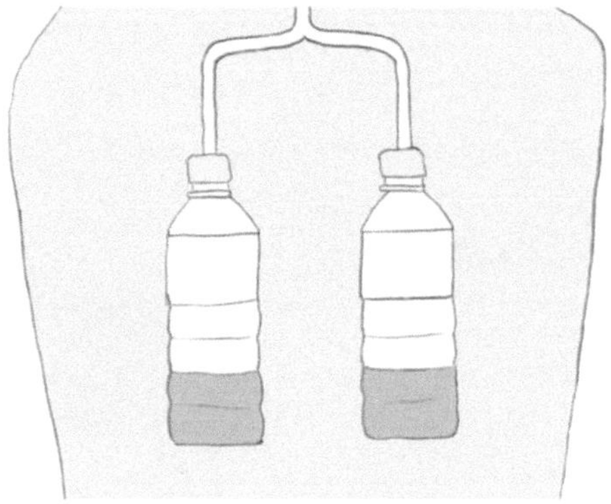

Image 8.8

There is an estimated 16 ounces of liquid in a healthy huwomxn's lungs.

Imagine a common occurrence when a person has a cold, and that person sneezes multiple times in a row with an uncovered or partially covered mouth. A series of 4–5 sneezes in a row can expel over one billion (1,000,000,000) flu viruses into the air in less than a minute.

Coughs and sneezes have different forces, with a cough having less force and traveling a shorter distance than a sneeze.

A cough has a speed of up to 50 miles per hour (mph). A sneeze is more powerful, with the liquid and air the lungs expel traveling at a speed of over 78 miles per hour (or 35 meters per second), and typically travels 6 feet to 26 feet (2 meters to 8 meters) merely from the force of the sneeze, without accounting for air circulation. Some studies estimate that the

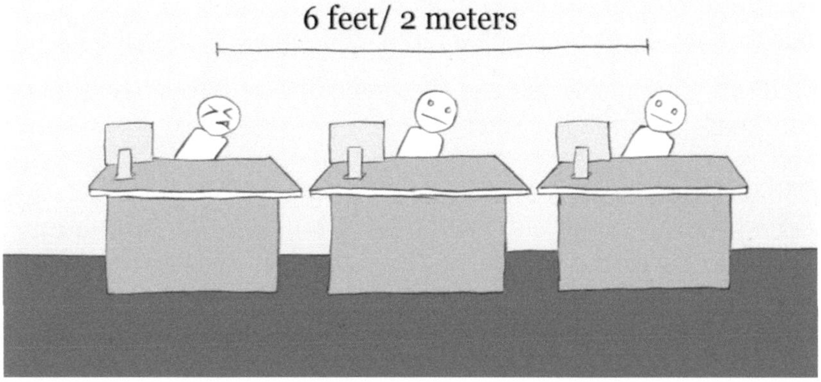

Image 8.9

The large virus-filled droplets which are expelled in a person's sneeze can travel over 78 mph and a distance of 6 to 26 feet from the force of the sneeze itself (without fans). That is the equivalent of two desks away.

numbers are on the lower end, with other research showing sneezes can travel 200 mph and further distances. This means that sneezes carry more flu virus microorganisms, quickly, to further distances than a cough.

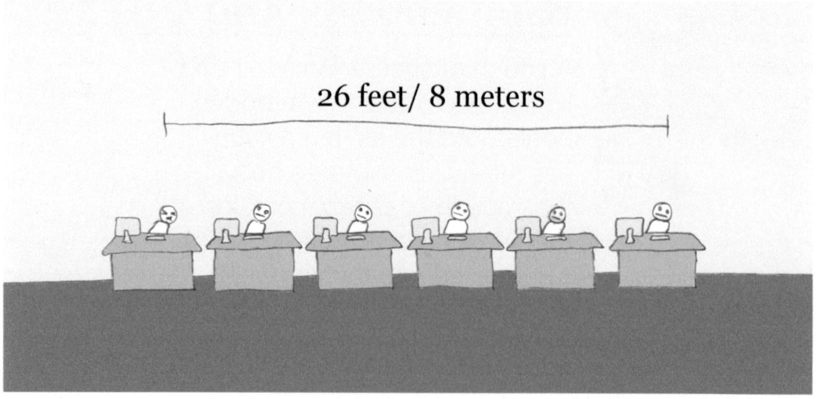

Image 8.10

A sneeze has smaller airborne droplets filled with the virus which can travel the length of five desks.

HOW VIRUSES MOVE THROUGH A SPACE

People inhale air and intake the particles in the air. This can include viruses that are in the air after a sneeze. Some airborne viruses that can move through the air after a sneeze include the chicken pox virus, measles, the common cold, and the flu (influenza).

Once in the air, the virus-infested air expands, with the snotty strings turning into droplets which move through the air. The droplets range in size, with the biggest droplets traveling up to 6 feet (2 meters) – the equivalent of two desks away in an office or classroom. The smaller droplets travel as far as 26 feet (8 meters) to as far as five desks away. In a few seconds they can spread through a room, and remain suspended for ten minutes.

The droplets from a sneeze can circulate in the air through a variety of means. In an outdoor space these can include wind, moving objects such as vehicles, people walking and stirring up the air and the viruses on surfaces, and touching a surface with a virus and

Image 8.11

Germs fill the air and rise upward towards the ventilation system and throughout the room filled with people.

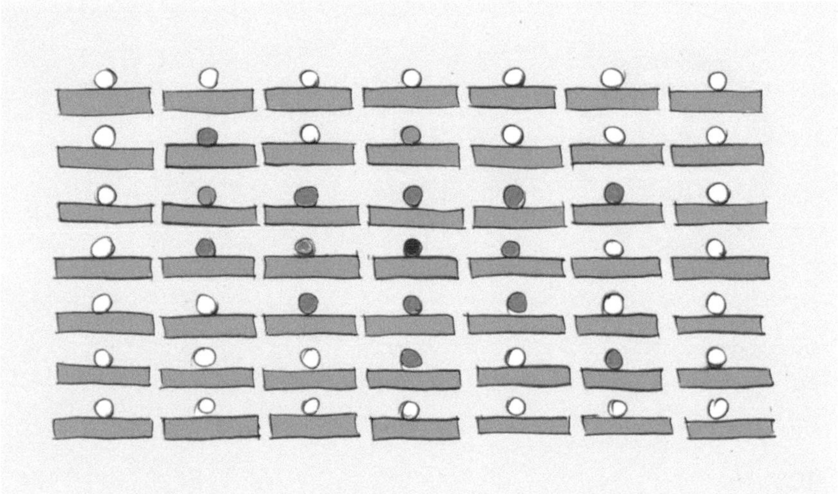

Image 8.12

One huwomxn's airborne virus (represented in the center dot in dark red) can infect 10–15% of people in an office in two weeks from coughs and sneezing (represented in lighter red).

moving it to another site. In an interior site there are open windows with wind blowing, vents, and ceiling and floor fans – all of which circulate contaminants in the air. People walk through spaces, waving their arms and picking up objects, all of which stir up air contami-*nants. People also* touch surfaces with the virus, moving the virus to additional surfaces in the space. Therefore, though the airborne virus may have settled on a surface, it can be made airborne again, and travel through building mechanical systems.

As the flu virus can still be infectious for 24 hours, the infectious virus can be circulating to multiple people walking in and out of the space, breathing the contaminated air or touching surfaces covered with the virus.

In outdoor areas there are larger ranges of space for the air to freely travel without structures to contain it. In interior air, there may be filters which the air circulates through. In commercial spaces high-efficiency particulate air (HEPA) filters (more on this in Chapter 10) may be installed, and perhaps regularly tested and replaced. However, many homes do not have a filtered air system. For those homes that do have one, routine testing and replacement of the filters may not be done as often as necessary to be effective in clearing contaminants from the air.

AIRBORNE FLU VIRUS INFECTIOUSNESS ON DIFFERENT SURFACES

Research for how long the flu virus remains viable in the air or on a surface has varied greatly in studies since the 1980s. This basic overview is given to help understand how the flu virus infectiousness can be reduced with the addition of living plant materials in a space.

Individuals with a flu infection can spread contagious viruses even before symptoms begin to appear. The virus structure degrades over time in the air or on a surface (when it is not inside a huwomxn). Once weakened, the virus is less able to attach to cells and spread its genetic mate-rial. Thus, the flu virus is reduced in infectiousness.

Image 8.13

The flu virus can be infectious for hours on some surfaces, such as desks, door handles, furniture handles, containers, appliances, and handrails. On steel surfaces, the flu virus is infectious for 24 hours.

The flu virus cannot bear the harsh conditions of the cold outside air. In 2011, the Public Health England researchers found that after nine hours the influenza A virus no longer has the capacity to infect people on most non-porous metal and plastic surfaces, such as aluminum and computer keyboards. On absorbent materials and fabrics, such as soft toys and wood surfaces, viable viruses disappeared after four hours.

In general, after 24 hours the flu virus is not viable on most surfaces. The *Famulari Theory* applications are for the more immediate virus which is expelled from sneezes and coughs, including those that are airborne, circulating through the air.

The rapid decrease in the flu virus infectiousness once outside the body is due to three main factors – the virus structure (not strong or stable), how much mucus surrounds the virus after the sneeze, and environmental conditions.

The focus on the environmental conditions is one which can be addressed in applications of the *Famulari Theory*. When exposed to different environments, the virus structure degrades or breaks down. Environmental conditions which directly weaken the flu virus are temperature, moisture, UV radiation from sunlight or artificial sources, pH change, and salt. With increased temperature, increased moisture from plant transpiration as well as from water features, and UV light from the sun and in the water features, the airborne virus is weakened through intentional green design.

HUMIDITY AND TEMPERATURE EFFECTS ON THE AIRBORNE FLU VIRUS – A STUDY

The study "High Humidity Leads to Loss of Infectious Influenza Virus from Simulated Coughs" by Noti et al., published in 2013, relates directly to adding increased humidity in a space to reduce the flu virus infectiousness.

The study addresses relative humidity (RH) in the space. Humidity is the amount of water vapor and water content in the atmosphere, while relative humidity is the percentage of water vapor at a given temperature. At greater temperatures, more humidity can be held in the air, such as in hot humid days of summer. At colder temperatures, the air cannot hold as much humidity, such as in cold dry winters. This study explores how humidity affects the infectiousness of the airborne flu virus.

> The researchers created an examination room that was 3.16 meters x 3.16 meters x 2.27 meters high (10 feet 4 inches x 10 feet 4 inches x 7 feet 5 inches high) and included a HEPA filter and an ultraviolet lamp to disinfect the chamber.
>
> **(Noti et al. 2013)**

> To access the effects of humidity on infectivity, influenza virus was coughed into a simulated examination room where the RH (relative humidity) was adjusted from 7–73%. The exam room contained coughing and breathing manikins facing each other and positioned 200 cm (approximately 6.56 ft) apart.
>
> **(Noti et al. 2013)**

All areas of the room were studied and found to have the same effective results. The viruses were collected in the room for five hours after the flu virus was coughed into the room. The results which relate to this research include:

> At low relative humidity, influenza retains maximal infectivity and inaction of the virus at higher relative humidity occurs rapidly after coughing. Although virus carried on aerosol particles greater than 4 microns have potential for remaining suspended in the air longer and traveling farther distances than those on larger particles, their rapid inactivation at high humidity tempers this concern. Maintaining indoor relative humidity greater than 40% will significantly reduce the infectivity of aerosolized virus.
>
> **(Noti et al. 2013)**

And finally, in 2010, the Hanley and Borup study of "Aerosol Influenza

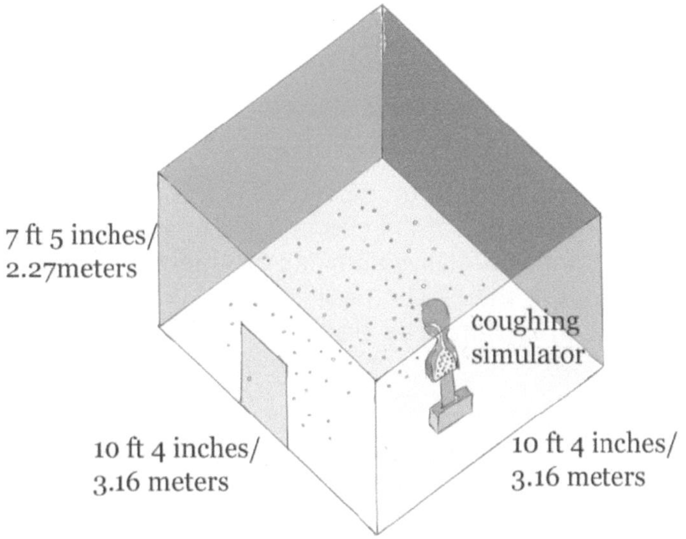

Image 8.14

A room 10 feet 4 inches x 10 feet 4 inches x 7 feet 5 inches high (3.16 meters x 3.16 meters x 2.27 meters high) with a coughing huwomxn form is used to study the effects of humidity to reduce the infectiousness of the flu virus.

Transmission Risk Contours: A Study of Humid Tropics Versus Winter Temperature Zone" examined

> aerosol transmissions of influenza for indoor locations frequented by jet travelers and developed risk contours for temperature and humidity that were based on studies reported in literature. They concluded that, in addition to intervention strategies including the use of masks and gloves, climate control of the indoor locations should be considered by public health planners in making recommendations to interrupt the spread of influenza.

In looking at applications of research for green site designs to reduce the infectiousness of the flu virus, an RH greater than 43% is five times more effective at reducing the flu viability than an RH of 7–23%.

PUTTING THE PIECES TOGETHER IN THE *FAMULARI THEORY*

In looking at these points directly as they apply to the *Famulari Theory* there are a few things to remember. First, the flu virus can be reduced in infectiousness in multiple ways while it is still airborne. The application of this with green site design proposes that with a higher temperature and higher relative humidity the flu virus will reduce its infectiousness.

Creating conditions that are comfortable for people to visit, work in, or live in can include creating a comfortable range of temperature with a minimum of 70°F and a comfortable relative humidity of a minimum of, or greater than 43%. Based on the study by Noti et al. (2013) an increase of temperature and relative humidity in this range reduced the infectiousness of the flu virus to less than 14.6–22.2%. Creating a balance of enough relative humidity to have an effect on the flu virus, but not too much for mold or the discomfort of huwomxns has been considered for each of the site designs.

In ideal conditions, plants can increase the water in the air (humidity) naturally, and additionally a water feature in the design will also increase the humidity of a space. In combination, temperature and relative humidity can reduce the airborne infectious flu. With the addition of plants with their trichomes (leaf hairs) the leaf surfaces act as a rough moist surface to hold the flu virus from air circulation. The placement of plants, relative to where people are in the space, is also important to reduce the infectiousness of the flu virus for people in the space.

Understanding research and studies which have been completed is needed in order to be creative in developing site applications for applying the research to green designs. In this chapter, understanding the flu virus structure, the ways in which the flu virus spreads once it is airborne, as well as research on RH and its effects on the virus helps to explain some of the pieces of the *Famulari Theory* and leads to the next elements of the fuller green theory.

REFERENCES

Greatorex, J. S., Page, R. F., Curran, M. D., Digard, P., Enstone, J. E., Wreghitt, T., Powell, P. P., Sexton, D. W., Vivancos, R., & Nguyen-Van-Tam, J. S. (2010). Effectiveness of common household cleaning agents in reducing the viability of human influenza A/H1N1. *PloS One*, *5*(2), e8987. doi:10.1371/journal.pone.0008987

Lange, N. R., & Schuster, D. P. (1999). The measurement of lung water. *Critical Care (London, England)*, *3*(2), R19–R24. doi:10.1186/cc342

McGill, K. (2018). Seasonal flu virus: Why vaccines never go out of style. *Sci, The Dish on Science*. https://thedishonscience.stanford.edu/posts/seasonalfluvaccine/ (retrieved 18 July 2020).

Noti, J. D., Blachere, F. M., McMillen, C. M., Lindsley, W. G., Kashon, M. L., et al. (2013). High humidity leads to loss of infectious influenza virus from simulated coughs. *PloS One*, *8*(2), e57485. doi:10.1371/journal.pone.0057485

Chapter 9

Plant Structure, Stomata, Transpiration, and Humidity

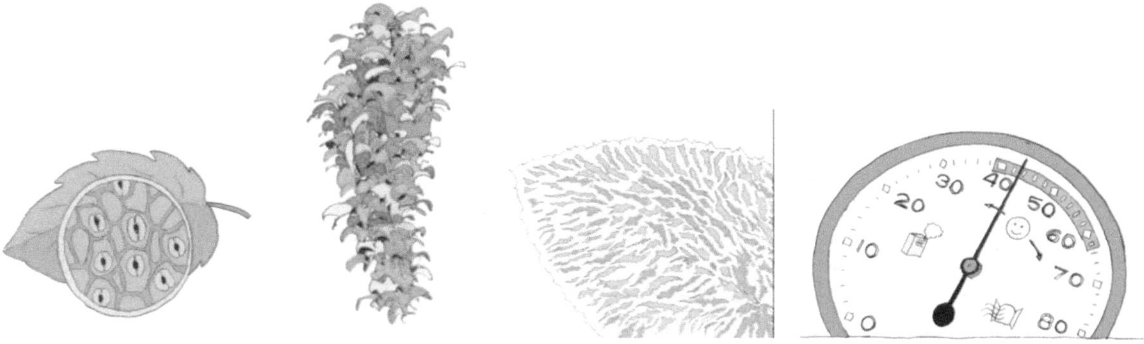

Image 9.1

The *Famulari Theory* has six pieces which reduce the infectiousness of airborne flu. In this chapter, the second element of stomata and transpiration, the third element of plant growth density, the fourth element of trichomes (plant hairs), and the fifth element of humidity are further explained.

PLANT STRUCTURE OVERVIEW

There are three basic parts of the plant to focus on for an understanding of this green theory – the roots below the ground, and the stem and leaves above the ground. The main root or primary root has additional smaller roots which grow outward and downward to stabilize the plant so the structure can grow over time to a fully mature plant. These smaller roots are called lateral roots. The roots also take in minerals and water from the soil which the plant needs to grow. Above the ground, the stem acts to carry the minerals and water to the leaves. Through the process of photosynthesis, the leaves take in energy from the sunlight to make food for the plant.

DOI: 10.4324/9781003136880-11

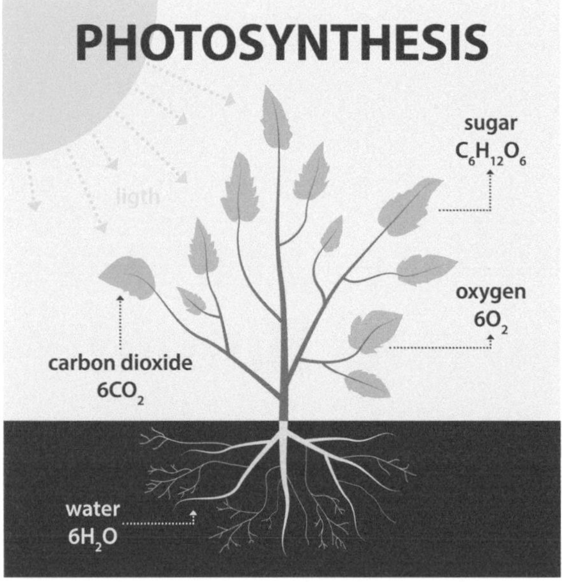

Image 9.2

Plant structure with photosynthesis.

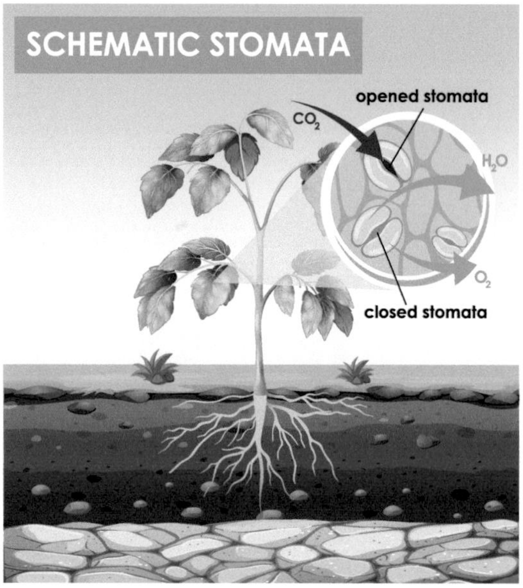

Image 9.3

Plant stomata on plant leaves.

The leaves of the plant are important for photosynthesis in collecting sunlight through the cells in the leaves. Carbon dioxide enters the plant through the stomata in the plant leaves. In photosynthesis, the plant uses carbon dioxide ($6CO_2$) and water ($6H_20$) to make sugars ($C_6H_{12}0_6$) and release oxygen (60_2). Through plant respiration the plant releases oxygen into the air. Huwomxns breathe in oxygen, and release carbon dioxide into the air.

The combination of water and minerals traveling from the roots in the ground to the stem and leaves is needed for the process of photosynthesis to take place successfully. Though plants evolve and adapt over time to their conditions, without any single one of these elements, sunlight, water, or minerals, the plant is not able to produce food, create oxygen, grow, produce flowers or fruit, or live.

DENSITY OF PLANT LEAVES

In looking at plants which are likely to be effective for reducing the

Image 9.4

Dense clumps of Calla leaves on a potted plant.

infectiousness of the airborne flu virus, choosing plants that have a dense cluster of leaves is one factor.

There is a variety of leaf shapes, sizes, and quantity in plants. One goal is to choose plants which have multiple leaves of medium or larger scale which overlap and layer other leaves on a plant. Picture plants which have only a few small leaves with lots of space to see through the leaves. Other plants have large dramatic leaves at the plant's edge, and very few leaves within the body of a plant. People can see many large gaps of space within the plant structure, and that indicates that the leaves do not have a dense leaf pattern or structure.

The ideal balance is choosing some plants which have medium or larger leaves, and whose leaves feel denser in their growth structure. This is so that the leaves act as a filter to hold the airborne viruses on their leaf surface.

The author, along with two researchers, Jen Russo and Amy Kerstetter, has developed a numerical rating system from 10 to 1 to rate the plants on their density of leaves in a typical mature living plant. The size of the leaf does not determine the density of its growth pattern. For a visual example of plant growth density, consider two people standing on opposite sides of the plant. When the two people look at each other, if all or much of their face is not visible because it is blocked with leaves, the plant is rated at 10 for density. In rating a plant with a 1, most or all of a person's face would visible if standing on opposite sides of the plant. The ratings between 10 and 1 relate to a range of visibility between each end of the spectrum.

TRICHOMES, PLANT HAIRS

Trichomes are the hairs on the surface of plant leaves and other parts of the plant. Some plants appear to have a waxy surface, while other plants appear to have a soft or fuzzy surface. The fuzzy surfaces are the trichomes. The trichomes, or plant hairs, can be in a pattern of single hairs, or can be branched in a pattern.

Trichomes can serve a few different roles in plants. Some trichomes prevent insects from getting to the surface of the leaf or plant to feed on. Trichomes of some plants contain types of chemical products which produce scent or flavor, such as in mint plants. One other role of the plant hairs is to shade the leaf so it can adjust to hotter climates.

Image 9.5

Trichomes on Lamb's Ear plant.

In addressing the *Famulari Theory*, choosing plants with trichomes on the leaf surface serves an important role. The airborne viruses are being circulated to the plants which have a fuzzy leaf surface to hold the virus in place, specifically, a more humid space on the leaf surface.. The surface of the plant leaf is a surface which can hold the airborne virus while it loses its infectiousness through humidity (including humidity produced by the plant at the leaf surface), temperature, and time. Plants with trichomes are more likely to have a surface which holds the virus more strongly than a waxy leaf. Even with a new light gust of air movement, the fuzzy leaf with a humid surface can hold the virus on the leaf.

Image 9.6

Close-up image of trichomes on *Cannabis indica* plant.

As with the plant growth density, the author, along with two researchers, Jen Russo and Amy Kerstetter, has developed a numerical rating system from 10 to 1 to rate the plants on their trichomes or how fuzzy a leaf appears due to the trichomes in a typical mature living plant. The length of the plant hair as well as the appearance of trichome density on the leaves or other surfaces of the plant both factor into the rating system. For example, if the leaf has plant hairs that appear soft to touch, as in petting a soft animal, it has a rating of 10 for trichomes. In rating a plant with a 1, the surface of the leaf feels waxy or has a texture of plastic. The ratings between 10 and 1 relate to a range of trichomes between each end of the spectrum.

PLANT STOMATA AND HOW THEY WORK

Plants have many stomata. "Stomata" is the plural for stoma, and the word most commonly used with plants. Plant stomata are the small microscopic membranes (openings) on a plant's surface which open and close, releasing water vapor into the air (which is called transpiration). Simply put, it is a natural process for a plant to take in water from the soil or air or water, and release some of that water back into the air through these pores in the plant. It may help to think of this as similar to a huwomxn drinking water throughout a day, and sweating part of the water out of their body through their pores.

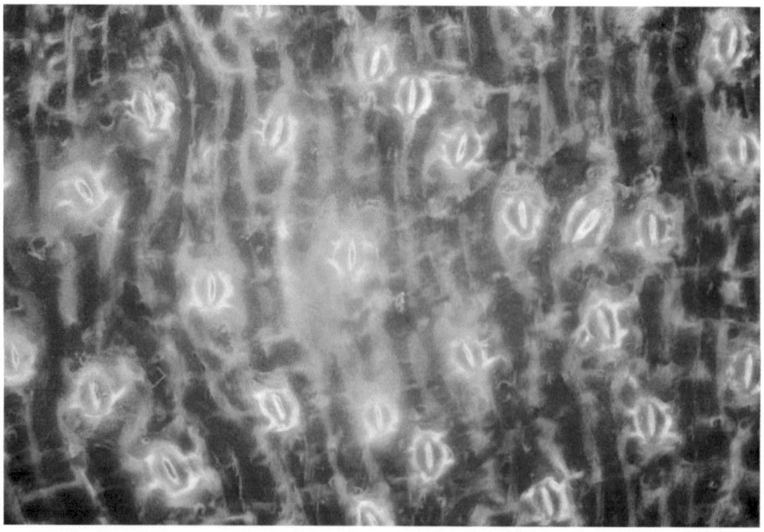

Image 9.7

Magnification of stomata on plant leaf.

Stomata are surrounded by a guard cell on each side. The guard cells change the shape to control the size of the stomata opening. It is the quantity and size of the stomata that affect the stomatal density and are important to address for application in the *Famulari Theory*.

Different plants (including trees, shrubs, perennials, grasses, etc.) have stomata on varying locations, including the top of the leaves, bottom of the leaves, needles, stem, and other organs. Plant stomata also vary in quantity on different plants.

Stomata on the plant surface are indicated in XX per square millimeter (mm), or XX mm^2. For understanding, there are 10 mm in 1 centimeter, and 25.4 mm in 1 inch.

All plants have stomata in order to absorb carbon dioxide (CO_2) for photosynthesis and release oxygen. Photosynthesis commonly occurs during the daytime when there is sunshine and carbon dioxide available for the plants to take in from the air through their stomata.

Some plants have more stomata on their leaves, for example, a water lily, or *Nymphaeaceae, which has stomata on the upper side of the leaves of about 460 mm^2. Nymphaeaceae grow in* water, and use the stomata on the upper side of the leaf for photosynthesis. Stomata on the underside of the leaf, where it is floating on the water, would serve no value to the plant.

The locations of the stomata on the plants are part of their structure as well as adaptations to their environment during their growth. In another example for understanding stomata, succulents have a low stomatal density in order to conserve water vapor and to be able to live in arid hot and dry conditions (Griffiths, 2017).

> Many succulents protect themselves further from water loss by working in the relative coolness of night; stomata open at night to take in CO2, and close during the hot, dry daytime, to conserve water loss. This requires a special adaption, though, because photosynthesis requires sunshine. These succulents have a way to rearrange CO2 molecules and store them overnight. When the sun comes up, the stomata snap shut, and the photosynthesis-engine starts, powered by the stored CO2.
>
> **(San Diego Zoo, n.d.)**

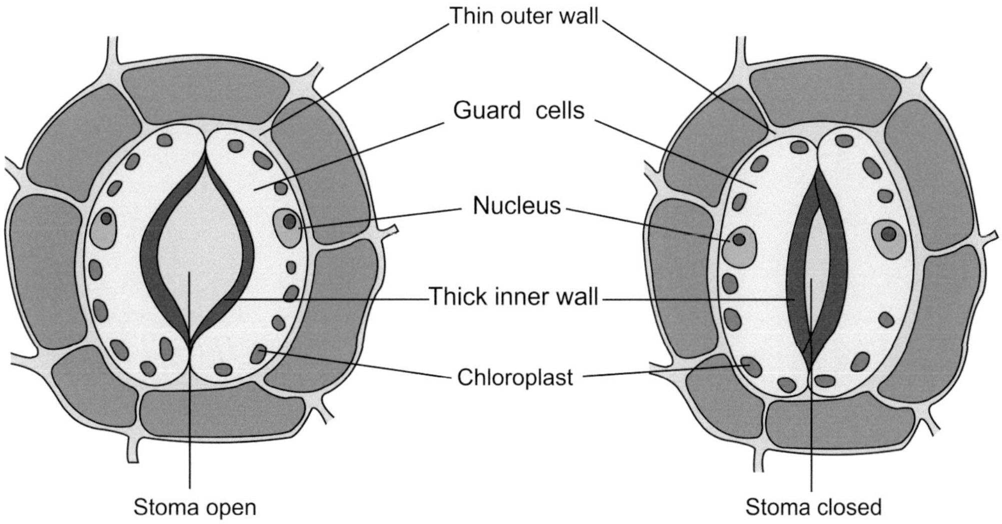

Image 9.8

Plant stomata in further detail.

Three of the most common environmental conditions which affect the opening or closing of stomata are light, water, and carbon dioxide concentration. Stomata open in light and moist conditions, and close in dark and dry conditions. Plant cells use carbon dioxide as part of the process of photosynthesis. With more people breathing in a space, as well as light and humidity, the environmental conditions promote stomata to open.

Image 9.9

Aloe Vera.

In relation to the *Famulari Theory*, understanding the stomata on plant leaves, and intentionally creating environmental conditions for stomata to open as well as seeking plants with more stomata on the leaf is beneficial in a few ways. Stomata release water vapor, which produces humidity, which reduces the infectiousness of the flu. Stomata also act as an open surface to hold the flu virus in place to make it unavailable to move throughout a space. If the virus cannot move through the air, then the virus is not available for huwomxns to become infected by.

Image 9.10

Areca Palm.

Plants for Use When Designing Green Spaces

Where People Are Resting at Night

Photosynthesis commonly takes place during the daytime, with sunshine and carbon dioxide (CO_2). At night during the dark hours, plants typically reverse this process and uptake oxygen and release CO_2. This process is called respiration.

Image 9.11

Peace Lily.

However, some plants can uptake carbon dioxide during the night as well because of their ability to perform a type of photosynthesis called Crassulacean Acid Metabolism (CAM). Having these plants at home improves air quality throughout the day and helps people to sleep better at night.

(Rawat, 2019)

Image 9.12

Snake Plant.

Image 9.13

Spider Plant.

These plants include:

- Aloe Vera, *Aloe barbadensis miller*
- Areca Palm, *Dypsis lutescens*

- Peace Lily, *Spathiphyllum* sp.
- Snake Plant, *Dracaena trifasciata*
- Spider Plant, *Chlorophytum comosum*
- Tulsi, also called Holy Basil, *Ocimum tenuiflorum*

Image 9.14

Tulsi.

Stomata on Plant Leaves

The plant takes in carbon dioxide to be used in photosynthesis through open stomata. Oxygen and water vapor are also released back into the air through open stomata.

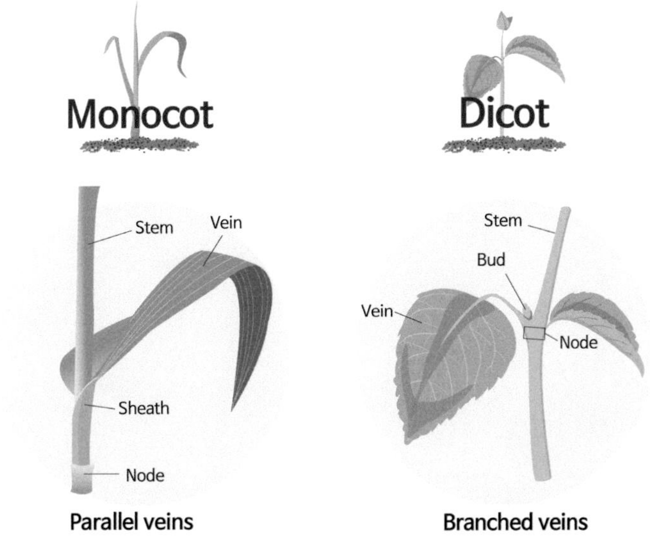

Image 9.15

Monocot and dicot leaves.

Green plants that reside on land typically have thousands of *stomata* on the surfaces of their leaves. The majority of stomata are located on the underside of plant leaves reducing their exposure to heat and air current. The chosen plants used in this green theory are those with stomata on the leaf surfaces – the top of the leaf, bottom of the leaf, or both sides of the leaf. Monocotyledon, or monocot for short, are plants which have stomata evenly distributed on both the top and bottom of the leaf surface. Dicotyledon, or dicot for short, are plants which have most stomata located on the bottom surface of the leaf.

Monocot and dicot plants can be visually identified in multiple ways. The simplest two ways are to look at the flowers and the leaves. In monocot plants, the flowers have petals in multiples of three (three, six, nine, etc.); whereas in dicot plants, the flowers have petals in multiples of four or five. In the leaves, the monocot plant has parallel, or up and down veins. The dicot leaves have scattered or netted markings – as in they do not follow any pattern. Visually, these two indicators are the easiest way to identify these classifications of plants.

Plants with high stomatal density, no matter their location on the leaf, are of more importance when applied to the *Famulari Theory* because they naturally release water into the environment and naturally remove airborne contaminants.

The choice to use plants with stomata on the leaf surfaces, including monocot plants when possible, is made for multiple reasons in the *Famulari Theory.* Stomata on the bottom of the leaf are suitable for use in the airborne flu virus, as circulation of the airborne contaminant can easily reach either side of the leaf. Also consider, the leaves of most plants are rarely strictly horizontal. Look around at plants and note the many different directions of plant leaves, revealing the top and bottom of the leaves in the same plant.

Why Plant Stomata Open and Close

There are conditions which make the stomata open or close.

> The opening and closing of stomata are regulated by factors such as light, plant carbon dioxide levels, and changes in environmental conditions. Humidity is an example of an environmental condition that regulates the opening or closing of stomata. When humidity conditions are optimal, stomata are open. Should humidity levels in the air around plant leaves decrease due to increased temperatures or windy conditions, more water vapor would diffuse from the plant into the air. Under such conditions, plant must close their stomata to prevent excess water loss.
>
> **(Bailey, 2019)**

For clarity in the *Famulari Theory*, the two basic conditions which are addressed in design which make stomata open are higher temperatures and higher humidity. Higher temperatures in the room or surrounding air open the pores, allowing water vapor to be released or transpire from the plant. Additionally, a higher humidity level in a room also makes plant stomata open, allowing them to release water. When stomata are open, the plants can take in available air contaminants, such as airborne car exhaust chemicals or other airborne contaminants.

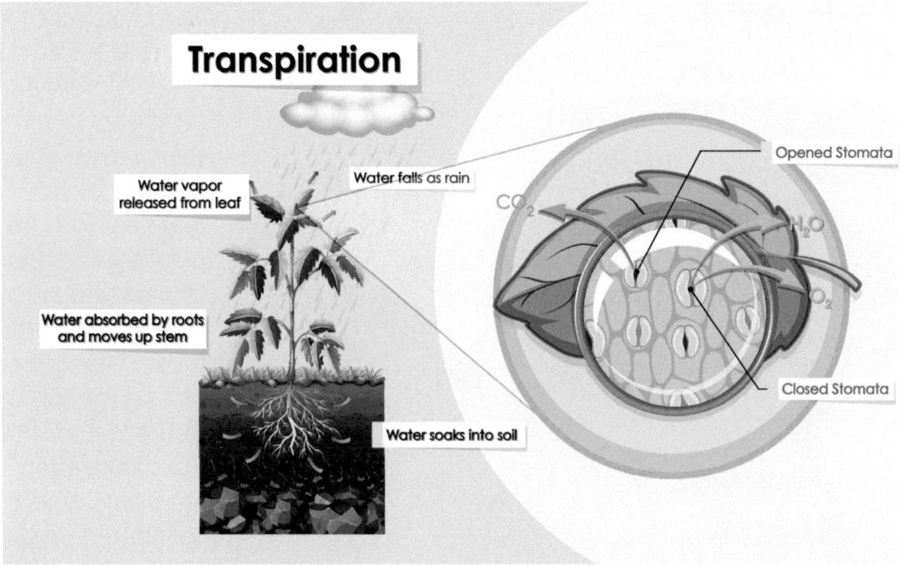

Image 9.16

Transpiration and stomata.

TRANSPIRATION – PLANTS RELEASE MOISTURE INTO THE AIR

Plants transpire water into the air, creating more humidity in the space. Think about it similarly to people transpiring, or perspiring or sweating water into the air. In a plant this is also called transpiration. This is beneficial for ease of breathing fresh air in both indoor and outdoor space. Transpiration is through the open stomata of the plants – taking in CO_2 and air moisture, and releasing oxygen as well water vapor into the air.

The water released from the plant leaves through transpiration accounts for 10% of the moisture in the atmosphere, globally (USGS, n.d.). Oceans, seas, and other bodies of water (lakes, rivers, streams, etc.) provide nearly 90% of moisture in the atmosphere. Transpiration rates vary widely depending on *weather conditions, such* as temperature, humidity and relative humidity, sunlight availability and intensity, precipitation, soil type and saturation, wind and air movement, plant types, and land slope (USGS, n.d.).

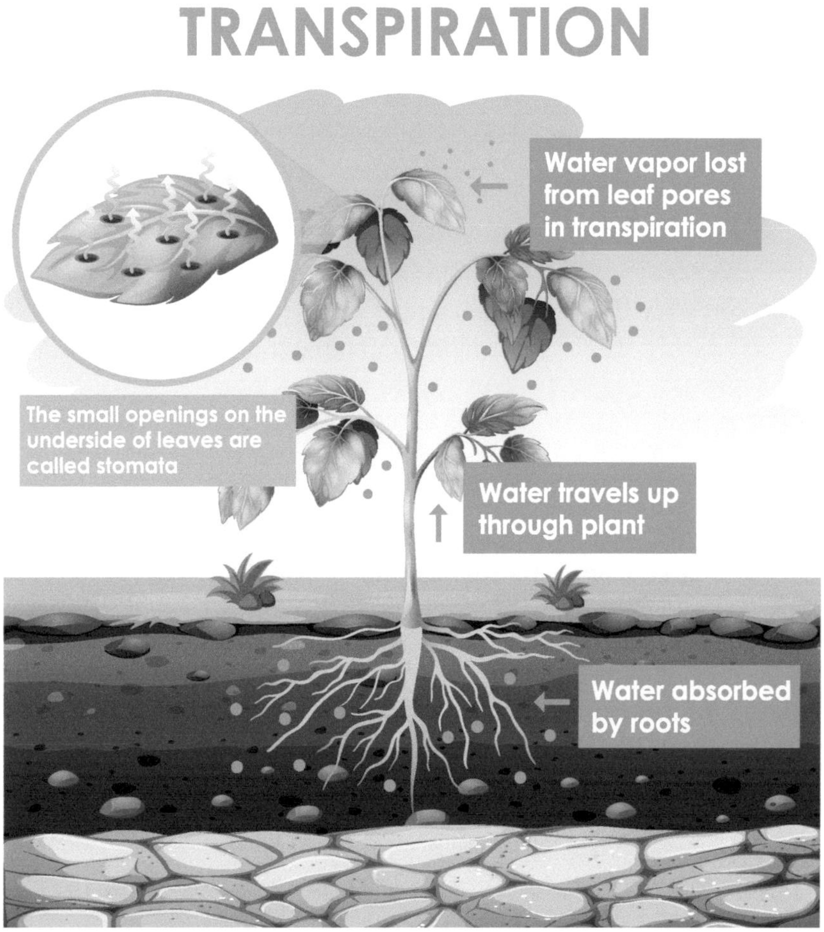

Image 9.17

Transpiration: water vapor released into the air.

During a growing season, plants will transpire more water than during a dormant season. Larger plants also produce more moisture into the air, such as a large oak tree which can transpire 40,000 gallons (151,000 liters) of water into the atmosphere. Water can evaporate not solely from plant leaves, but also from the soil in the vicinity of the plants, as well as from water elements in the space. Plants only use a small percentage of water for growth and biological processes. More than 90% of water is lost through transpiration and released back into the air.

Image 9.18

Bamboo Palm.

Image 9.19

Boston Fern.

In a smaller space, such as parks, or interior spaces, plants can have a larger direct effect on the humidity in the air. Enclosed spaces can act as their own controlled

Image 9.20

Kimberly Fern.

microclimate. In interior spaces, huwomxns can control the light, temperature, and air circulation. With this knowledge, people can consciously create a space which has a specific range of humidity through plants, and water features.

Image 9.21

Dwarf Banana.

As written in Chapter 8, there is a study which states that with higher humidity and temperatures the flu virus was reduced in infectiousness. This is significant in designing spaces which have plants which can help add humidity to the air.

An approach to adding humidity through water vapor is through choosing plants which have higher transpiration rates. Author and researcher B.C. Wolverton has studied the use of plants to remove contaminants from the air (phytoremediation) and has written extensively on his studies. His research of plants with high transpiration includes these plants, as well as others:

Image 9.22

Florist's Mum.

- Acer Palm, *Chrusalidocarpus lutescens*
- Bamboo Palm, *Chamaedora seifrizii*
- Boston Fern, *Nephrolepsis exaltata "Bostoniensis"*
- Kimberly Queen Fern, *Nephrolepsis obliterata*
- Lady Palm, *Rhapis excelsa*
  - Ficus Alii, *Ficus macleilandii "Allii"*
  - Peace Lily, *Spathiphyllum* sp.
  - Florist's Mum, *Chrysanthemum morifolium*
  - Gerbera Daisy, *Gerbera jamesonii*
  - Dracena "Warneckei," *Dracena deremensis "Warnecki"*
  - Dwarf Banana, *Musa cavendishii*

Image 9.23

Gerbera Daisy.

Some of the plants used in the example site designs are based on the research of B.C. Wolverton. He rated plants in his studies from 10 to 1, with 10 having high transpiration rates (such as an Acer Palm) and 1 having a low transpiration rate. All plants from his publications have been reviewed for the *Famulari Theory.* Some plants with high transpiration rates have been noted in the database of the *Famulari Theory* located at www.steviefamulari.net/Famulari-Theory.

HUMIDITY LEVELS

The comfortable level of relative humidity is balanced with the comfortable temperature of the room. In understanding humidity in design, there is also the term relative humidity which needs clarification.

An overview of humidity requires an understanding between the relationship of temperature and the moisture in the air – the humidity levels. At lower temperatures, the air cannot hold as much moisture. Whereas, with higher temperatures, typically, the air can hold a larger amount of moisture.

You may recall being in a room that feels too dry and uncomfortable to breathe, no matter the room temperature. Or perhaps you may be in a winter season in New York where it is cold and dry, making it uncomfortable to breathe. Equally, you may have been in spaces that have a high level of humidity, thus making it challenging to breathe.

Some amount of humidity is needed for comfort for breathing. Between temperature and humidity, there is a balance for each space, as well as for the use and design of it.

Humidity is the water content of the mixture of water vapor and other elements found in the air; while relative humidity is the percentage of water vapor in the air at a given temperature. In other words, humidity is how much "air" is in the air versus the amount of water. Relative humidity (RH) however, takes the humidity ratio, and includes the air temperature, and the maximum amount of water the air can hold, and displays it as a percentage. The RH is expressed as a percent and also measures water vapor, but relative to the temperature of the air.

Simply put, RH is a measure of the actual amount of water vapor in the air compared to the total amount of vapor that can exist in the air at its current temperature. Warmer air can hold more water vapor, and therefore its relative humidity is less than the same air sample at a lower temperature. The lower temperature air will feel drier.

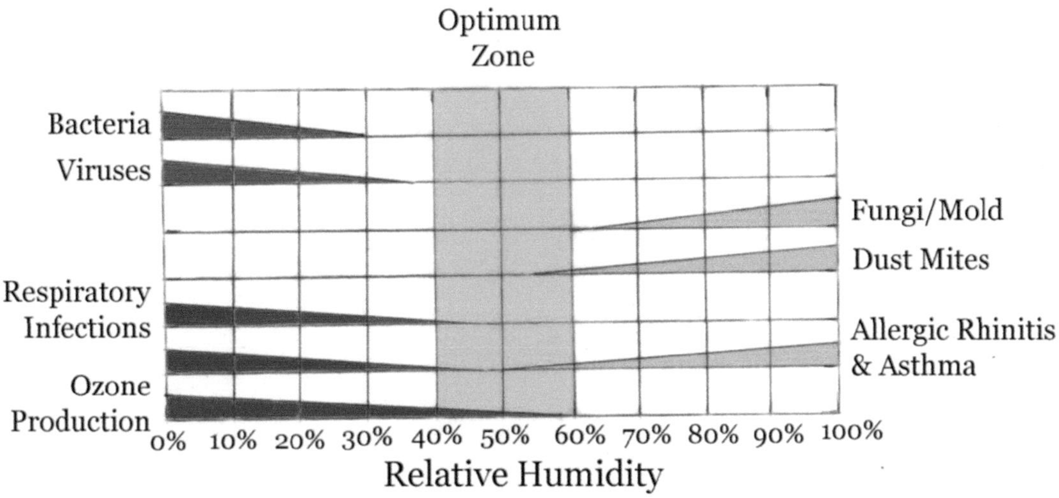

Image 9.24

Chart of relative humidity and its relationship to other conditions.

Warmer air will increase the drive for transpiration in plants, whereas colder air will reduce the drive for transpiration.

Designing to Increase Relative Humidity

Briefly explained, there are four basic factors which are important for people to be comfortable in a space – temperature, relative humidity, air movement, and mean radiant temperature.

> Temperature – how hot or cold is it? Huwomxns like to be in the range of 70 to 80 degrees Fahrenheit (21.1–26.67 degrees Celsius) more or less. This is the most basic factor for comfort.
>
> Relative humidity – how much moisture is in the air? Forty to sixty percent relative humidity is the ideal range.
>
> Air movement – is the air moving across your skin? In the summer, one way that our bodies keep cool is by the evaporation of sweat. A nice breeze or a ceiling fan can keep us comfortable even when the temperature and humidity are at or above the narrow range we find most comfortable.
>
> Mean Radiant Temperature. How hot or cold are the surfaces around you? Of the four factors of comfort, this one's the least recognized or understood, but let me give you a couple of examples. If you've ever been in an old uninsulated house with single pane windows on a cold night, you've probably experienced discomfort due to a low mean radiant temperature. The cold inner wall surfaces and glass suck heat out of your body because you're radiating heat to them but they're not radiating much back. Another mean radiant temperature problem occurs in bonus rooms, where you have walls with [a] hot attic on the other side. Most of the time those attic kneewalls are poorly insulated and thus get very hot. Even if the air temperature in that room is 70 degrees, you may be uncomfortable because the walls keep blasting you with heat.
>
> **(Bailes, 2010)**

The first three factors – temperature, humidity, and air movement – are applied to the site designs in the *Famulari Theory*.

Plants are one source for adding humidity to a space. There are humidifiers and vaporizers to add humidity to the air. Creating a high enough humidity which

1. Encourages the plants stomata to open
2. Reduces flu virus infectiousness
3. Is at a comfortable level for people to be in the room – is all a balance

A hydrometer is used for measuring the humidity and relative humidity of a space. These range in price and accuracy depending on the model.

In determining the RH of a space, one must consider the use of the space. For example, in the summertime along the ocean, some people enjoy the heat and humidity. However, that same temperature and relative humidity are uncomfortable for indoor living conditions.

Image 9.25

Visible humidity inside window.

Grouping plants together, especially ones with high transpiration rates, will create a more humid microclimate. Larger leaves allow plants to absorb more light and carbon dioxide (CO_2) in photosynthesis, and allow for more water loss into the atmosphere. For the *Famulari Theory*, this is directly applicable.

In looking at locations for interior plants, putting plants near where people sit or stand is beneficial for adding humidity to the air. The amount of humidity produced from plants in a room does not travel far from the location of the group of plants. Higher humidity reduces the infectiousness of the flu (based on the study discussed in Chapter 8). Therefore, designing for people to be closer to the plants with the higher relative humidity is beneficial in these designs. Not putting a plant directly underneath a vent, so that the open vent sucks the water vapor out of the space, is a basic understanding of healthcare for plants.

Designing for a balance of comfort for the people who use the space, as well as for reduction of *infectiousness of the flu virus, as well as for creating an ideal range for plant stomata to open* – that is the range which is explored in the *Famulari Theory*, and specific for each site.

PUTTING THE PIECES TOGETHER IN THE *FAMULARI THEORY*

The basic searches for plants include plant zone, size, growth rate, color of leaves or flowers, etc. To make it easier for readers, I have included plants names and photographs in the earlier chapters for each site design. The plants in the site designs are chosen for a variety of reasons. Directly for the *Famulari Theory*, I rate plants for their stomatal density, trichomes density, and density of leaf growth. Other conditions include natural light availability, plant zones, color, scale, plant growth, and other reasons. There are also aesthetic reasons to choose different plants.

Looking for plants that have a high stomatal density on their leaf surface is not a traditional way to search for plants. However, due to the importance of choosing plants with clumps of dense leaves, larger leaf surfaces, and large density of stomata on the leaves, I have specifically addressed this in choosing plants for the site designs based on their stomata per square millimeter on the leaf surface, when the information is available. Plant studies have not been published on all plants to determine their stomata density. The stomata and transpiration of the plants is a notable part of the consideration and therefore a great amount of consideration is put into choosing plants that support the *Famulari Theory*.

Further considerations in plant choices include plants with visible trichomes (hairs on the leaf surface). With the hairs on the plant leaves, there are more rough surfaces which allow the viruses to be held in without movement. Additionally, open stomata and densely grown leaves of plants act as a surface for holding the airborne viruses. The viruses which are circulating in the air can get trapped on the leaf surface, thus making it more challenging to circulate. This is beneficial for people.

With the virus not circulating in the air, instead lying on the leaf surface or in the stomata, the virus becomes unavailable for huwomxn access. Thus, this reduces some of the ability of the flu to infect people. A resource for the plants used in this green theory can be found on a database at www.steviefamulari.net/Famulari-Theory.

REFERENCES

Bailes, A. (2010, 7 June). The 4 factors of comfort. *Energy Vanguard.* https://www.energyvanguard.com/blog/24336/The-4-Factors-of-Comfort (retrieved 22 August 2020).

Bailey, R. (2019, August 15). What is the function of plant stomata? *Thoughts Co.* https://www.thoughtco.com/plant-stomata-function-4126012 (retrieved 2 August 2020).

Griffiths, H., & Males, J. (2017). Succulent plants. *Current Biology, 27*(17), R890–R896. doi:10.1016/j.cub.2017.03.021

San Diego Zoo. (n.d.). Cactuses and succulents. *San Diego Zoo.* https://animals.sandiegozoo.org/plants/cactuses-succulents (retrieved 22 August 2020).

United States Geological Survey (USGS). (n.d.). Evapotranspiration and the water cycle. https://www.usgs.gov/special-topic/water-science-school/science/evapotranspiration-and-water-cycle?qt-science_center_objects=0#qt-science_center_objects (retrieved 4 June 2020).

Chapter 10

Putting the Pieces Together for Living Green Design in the *Famulari Theory*

CIRCULATING AIR THAT HAS VIRUSES THROUGH PLANTS

Air circulation is the final aspect of the *Famulari Theory*. Viruses that are in the air need to gently circulate to a plant's surface. Air circulation applications for this green theory truly are that simple. When the influenza virus is in the moisture-rich air, plants can take the moisture into the plant or soil and use the moisture for photosynthesis. This process repeats over and over as the plant continues to grow.

Circulation may require mechanical fans such as ceiling fans, floor fans, vents, or natural cross-ventilation of wind to move or circulate air. The contaminated air must move to the plants in order for it to effectively filter the air contaminants, in this case the flu virus. Air circulation can

Image 10.1

The *Famulari Theory* has six pieces which reduce the infectiousness of the airborne flu. In this chapter, air circulation is further explained, as well as putting all the pieces of the theory together.

DOI: 10.4324/9781003136880-12

be used to push and pull air through a space. In a simple example, this is commonly shown in cross-ventilation with windows on opposite sides of a room open and the breeze that moves through both, such as Image 10.4.

Air Circulation in Outdoor Spaces

In outdoor settings wind moves through a space, creating movement in the air. Buildings, structures, trees, and plants alter wind patterns.

> Wind patterns change based on structures. When I lived in Fargo, North Dakota one alley routinely had a noticeable wind tunnel and even had a large gathering of snow during the winter season. The snow drift was an indicator that the buildings were altering the wind pattern such that the force of the wind was stronger in that area of the wind tunnel.
>
> Essentially, wind moves naturally, hits an unmovable source such as [a] row of buildings along a block, the wind finds a gap of an alley between buildings and the wind goes in it strongly, then is caught in the alley with the snow it was carrying. The wind carries the snow to the alley along the side of the building, and deposits it there. Some of the wind escapes the alley. This is felt when you walk across the front of it feeling a large gust of wind that is not as strong in other areas along the same block.
>
> **(Famulari, 2020)**

Image 10.2

Plants are natural air purifiers. Air which has contaminants and has then been circulated through plants, either by the wind or by mechanical means, has reduced contaminants and is cleaner.

The same applies to the air when there is not snow, but rather just wind with airborne flu contaminants.

> Wind also carries air and all that is in it. Whether it is forceful wind or gentle wind, air is moved throughout short and long distances. There are items which create wind, such as a moving truck. If driving in a small car and a large truck has driven by you, you have likely felt the force of the moving truck. It is not just weather that creates wind, but also moving forces. For those of you that have experiences seeing the fur of their pet floating in the air, then sitting on the wood floor, then moving in the air again when you walk by it, causing enough of a movement from your foot nearby it for it to again move into the air and land a few feet away. Some contaminants in the air can be understood the same way.
>
> **(Famulari, 2020)**

This information addresses the fact that air moves, and the contaminants in the air moves with it. The airborne flu virus will travel for multiple feet from the outdoor wind.

Air Circulation in Interior Spaces

In interior spaces, open windows create cross-ventilation, with one window pushing fresh air through, while the other window takes stale air out. Though both open windows will both push air and pull air – in combination both windows allow circulation more effectively.

Image 10.3

Indoor ventilation and droplets airborne transmission of viruses.

With the addition of fans on both the ceiling and the floor, as well as air vents and open windows in a space, air circulation can be directed through a space in a healthy pattern for fresh air.

The *Famulari Theory* addresses air circulation with the airborne flu virus through plants. The plants, specifically the leaves, act as a living filter which holds the airborne virus on the leaf surface, thus preventing the virus from continuing to move through the air. The leaf, with its trichomes (plant hairs) and open stomata, creates a living moist space for the virus to sit and reduce its infectiousness. The transpiration from the plant leaf creates a small area of higher humidity around the leaf and plants, as well affecting the larger space of the room.

Image 10.4

Apartment ventilation system.

MERV AND HEPA FILTERS EXPLAINED

Filters in interior spaces are designed to remove contaminants from the air. Minimum efficiency reporting value (MERV) was created in 1987 to report the effectiveness of air filters. HEPA is an acronym for "high-efficiency particulate air" and is used as an efficiency standard of air filters. It was commercialized in the 1950s after being developed during World War II for gas masks. The effectiveness of air filters is based on the size of the particle it can filter from the air.

MERV ratings of air filters are in Image 10.6, ranging from MERV 1 to 20.

MERV ratings of filters are in the following ranges:

MERV 1–4 low quality
MERV 5–12 medium quality
MERV 13–20 high quality
MERV 17–20 high HEPA filter of 99.97%

MERV 1–4 are commonly found in use and have an efficiency value of less than 35% for air particles 3 to 10 microns in range. This means that more than 65% of these air particles pass through the filter without being captured. The filters which range from MERV 5 to 8 are also commonly found for purchase of air systems and have a large range of 20% to 70% effectiveness at filtering out small air contaminants. MERV 9 is recommended for homes due to the family needs, range of ages, health, and guests. MERV 13–20 are HEPA filters used typically in hospitals, nursing homes, and gaseous buildings.

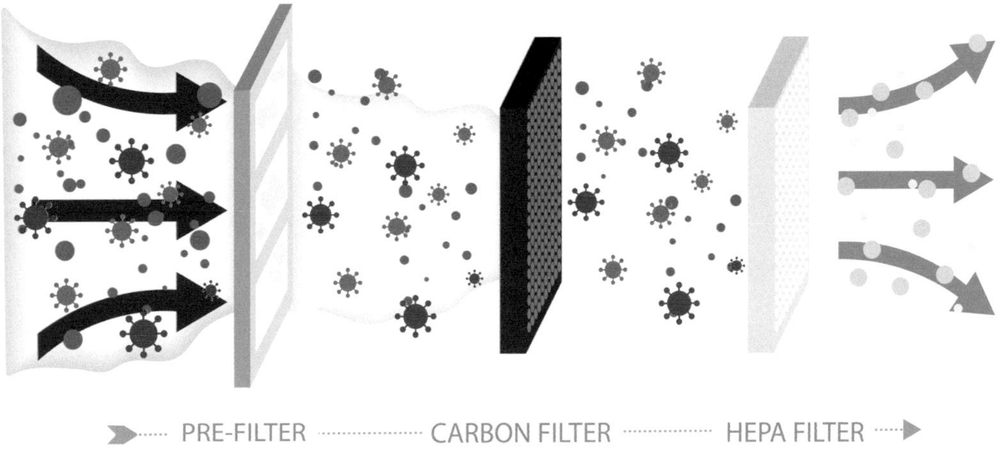

Image 10.5

Air purification and filtration process by passing through pre-filter, carbon, and HEPA.

Ratings	0.3 - 1 microns	1 - 3 microns	3 - 10 microns	Filter Type	Controlled Particles
MERV 1	-	-	<20%	Pre-filter/ Aluminum Mesh	Dust, dust mites, pet dander, pollen
MERV 2	-	-	<20%		
MERV 3	-	-	<20%		
MERV 4	-	-	<20%		
MERV 5	-	-	20-34%	Low quality MERV filter	Mold, spores, cooking dust, hair spray
MERV 6	-	-	35-49%		
MERV 7	-	-	50-69%		
MERV 8	-	<20%	<70%		
MERV 9	-	<35%	<35%	Standard MERV filter	Lead dust, smaller mold, smaller pollen
MERV 10	-	50-64%	<75%		
MERV 11	<20%	65-79%	<80%		
MERV 12	<35%	80%	<85%		
MERV 13	<50%	<90%	<90%	Superior MERV filter	Bacteria, viruses, fine dust
MERV 14	75-84%	<90%	<90%		
MERV 15	85-94%	<90%	<90%		
MERV 16	<95%	<95%	<95%		
MERV 17	99.97%	<99%	<99%	HEPA filter	Small bacteria and viruses, fumes
MERV 18	99.97%	<99%	<99%		
MERV 19	99.97%	<99%	<99%		
MERV 20	99.99997%	<99%	<99%		

Image 10.6

This chart illustrates the minimum efficiency reporting value (MERV) rating system created in 1987. The MERV system reports the effectiveness of air filters as well as what size and type of particle the filter is able to remove from the air. (AirFuji, n.d.)

There are numerous companies which produce air filters. Some air filters are permanent and require cleaning the filter every 30 days. Most air filters however are disposed of every month to six months (depending on the site use, site users, quantity of users, and other conditions). Air filters are less effective over time as they are being exposed to the air contaminants and the filter continues to gather air particulate matter in the medium. Air filters may contain synthetic filtering media, fiberglass, aluminum, activated carbon, and other numerous materials (Eldman, 2009). Disposed-of air filters are added to the landfill, adding a continued detrimental impact on the environment.

Image 10.7

One type of house ventilation.

Effectiveness of Air Filters and Air Ventilation

Ventilation systems are used for filtering air for cooling a space, heating a space, or both. The *Famulari Theory* can support and work in conjunction with a HEPA and other filtering systems.

Air filters used in residential and commercial buildings are discarded with waste. The particles which were trapped in the filters can be again released into the air, water, or ground while in a landfill. This cycle is not sustainable or beneficial for long-term improvement of air quality.

Filters lose their effectiveness in filtering air particles based on the age of the filter, a greater quantity of users of the space, and different users of the space that the ventilation was not originally intended for. Some examples of users who produce more contaminants which get trapped in the air filter include smokers, artists who use powders or aerosols, and manufacturers of products which generate dust and air particles during the creation of their product.

Multiple factors play a role in a less than fully effective ventilation system. These include

Image 10.8

Warehouse ventilation.

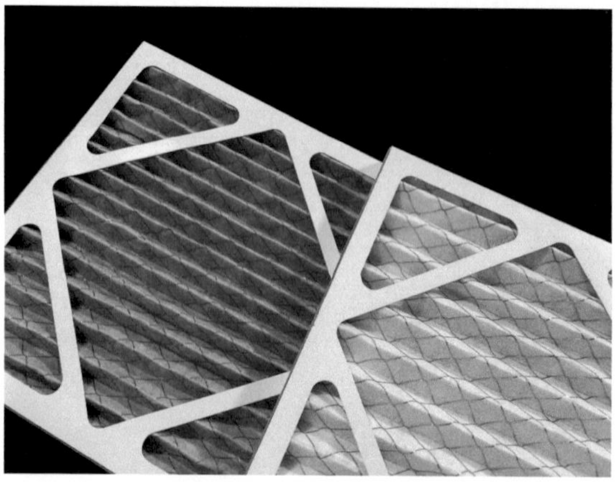

Image 10.9

HVAC air filters, after use and clean.

outdated ventilation system designs, the filters not being changed as frequently as appropriate, new viruses since the design or filter was developed, change of use of the space, and more people using the space more frequently. Some ventilation systems may not be effective for new airborne viruses and other contaminants.

Another factor which affects the air contaminants is the age of the building. Older buildings were created with materials which can be harmful to people due to the off-gassing of their decaying materials, or simply put, because the materials are naturally breaking down. These buildings can produce air contaminants as they age. These air contaminants then add to the mix of air which the air filters trap. The room may not be sustainable long term if air ventilation is not addressed. Due to these factors, the room may become a part of the issue of SBS and sick rooms.

Sick Building Syndrome

SBS is one factor in reduced health of people.

> The sick building syndrome comprises of various nonspecific symptoms that occur in the occupants of a building. This feeling of ill health increases sickness absenteeism and causes a decrease in productivity of the workers. As this syndrome is increasingly becoming a major occupational hazard, the cause, management and prevention of this condition are discussed in this article.
>
> **(Joshi, 2008)**

> The sick building syndrome (SBS) is used to describe a situation in which the occupants of a building experience acute health- or comfort-related effects that seem to be linked directly to the time spent in the building. No specific illness or cause can be identified. The complainants may be localized in a particular room or zone or may be widespread throughout the building.
>
> **(EPA, n.d.)**

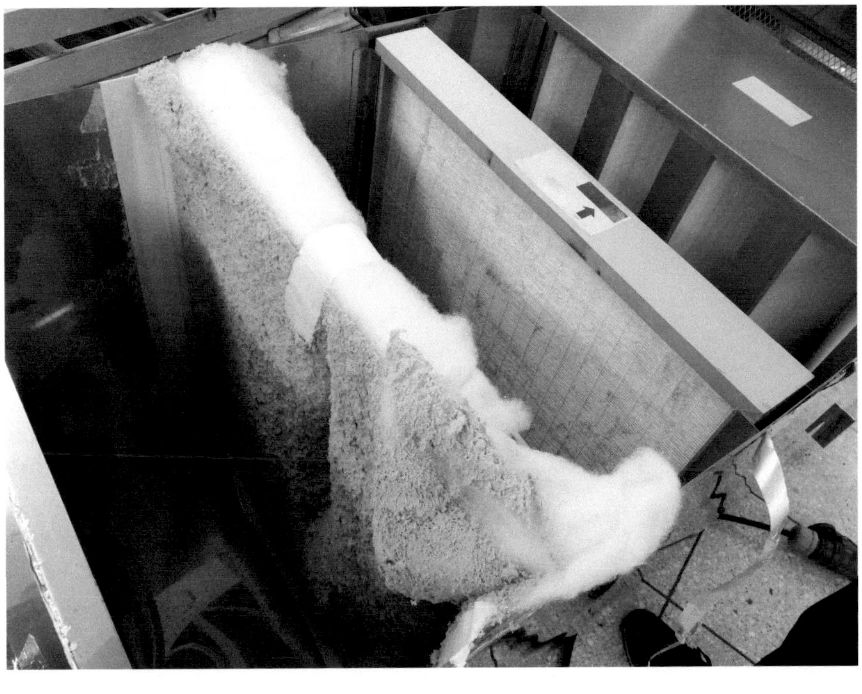

Image 10.10

Pre-filter, medium filter, and HEPA filter of vacuum cleaners for air duct cleaning.

Two of the sources of SBS include inadequate ventilation and low humidity.

In addressing inadequate ventilation, there is the example below:

In 1970, oil embargo led building designers to make buildings more airtight, with less outdoor air ventilation, in order to improve energy efficiency. (NSC, n.d.) The ventilation was reduced to 5 cfm/person. This reduced ventilation rate was found to be inadequate to maintain the health and comfort of building occupants. Malfunctioning heating, ventilation and air-conditioning systems (HVAC systems) also increase the indoor air pollution.

In order to have an acceptable indoor air quality (IAQ) with a minimum energy consumption, The American Society of Heating, Refrigeration and Air-Conditioning Engineers (ASHRAE) recently revised ventilation standards to a minimum outdoor air flow rate of 15 cfm/person to avoid the problems related to inadequate ventilation. The standards are 20 cfm/person in office spaces and 60 cfm/person in smoking lounges.

Poor design and construction of buildings with more number of offices cramped in a building to increase the salable area also contribute to inadequate ventilation.

(EPA, n.d.)

Poor and inappropriate lighting with the absence of sunlight, bad acoustics, poor ergonomics, and humidity may also contribute to SBS.

The symptoms of SBS are commonly seen in people with clerical jobs than in people with managerial jobs because professionals or managers have better working conditions. The symptoms are more common in females than in males probably because more females are in secretarial jobs, they are more aware of their health or a lesser dose of pollutants is required to manifest the effects. The symptoms are more common in air-conditioned buildings than in naturally ventilated buildings and are more common in a public sector building than in a private sector building.

(Joshi, 2008)

Comfort levels recommended by the Chartered Institution of Building Services Engineers (CIBSE 1986) include:

- Temperature of 66–73°Fahrenheit, 19–23°Celsius
- Relative humidity (RH) of 40–70%
- More than 55% RH is needed in carpeted buildings with underfloor heating to avoid electrostatic shocks (Joshi, 2008)

Ventilation of fresh air is determined in terms of the quantity of fresh air delivered per person. Further calculations to deliver more fresh air are needed in places where there are people who smoke.

In addition to the quantity of fresh air, the speed at which the air is exchanged in a space is part of a design of a space. When air is not exchanged frequently enough it causes stuffiness, and when exchanged too quickly it feels draughty. These are some of the elements in designed spaces which can affect SBS, most of which can be improved with more conscious and considerate design.

THE *FAMULARI THEORY* AND FILTERS – A COMBINATION

Applications of the *Famulari Theory* help support the current ventilation systems of buildings which have effective and ineffective ventilation and air circulation. In spaces which have ineffective ventilation or air circulation, or do not have any air filtering system, the applied *Famulari Theory* takes on a more important role for the health of the space.

Newer houses are designed with ventilation systems for heating and cooling in which owners are responsible for changing the filters. Owners may not use proper air filters or may not change

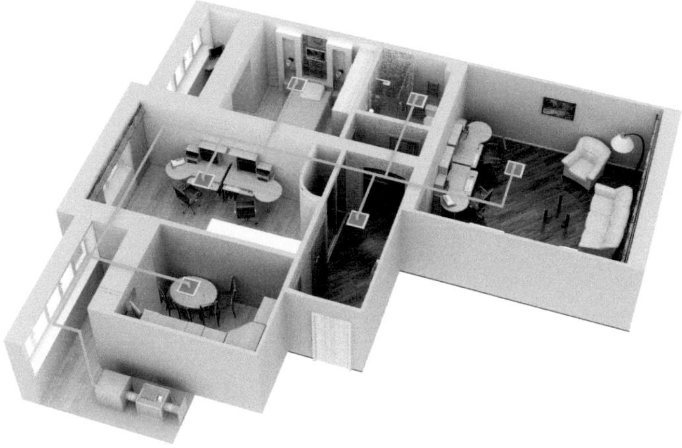

Image 10.11

Apartment ventilation system.

the filters often enough to be effective. Some older homes may not have filtered air systems and it may be difficult to renovate to create one. Some apartments do not have air filters, particularly older apartments. Though an apartment building may have ventilation for the common areas, individual apartments have windows and ceiling fans for ventilation but not filtered air through a system. Open windows for cross-ventilation are one approach users can take for fresh air in lieu of air filters.

In warehouses where people work, there may not be effective HEPA filters for ventilation systems for improving air quality. The temperature of the warehouses may be lower than 70°F. Though the air temperature may need to be low for the items being stored, the workers who are routinely in the space are exposed to low temperatures and ineffective air ventilation that may not be designed primarily for the health of the workers.

Air filtration systems of office buildings vary greatly depending on the age of the building and use of the space. As businesses change in an office building, air ventilation system filters may no longer be effective for the next use of the space. Additionally, the quality of filters varies greatly such as more highly effective filters being changed to less effective filters without full consideration of the users, air exchange flow, and other factors.

The intentions of the *Famulari Theory* are to not only stand by itself as green design to reduce the infectiousness of the airborne flu virus but also to improve air quality. This research also supports working with existing air filters and air circulation and ventilation systems. Combining both the green practices of the *Famulari Theory* along with current air filtration systems when possible is more effective than either one by itself.

In places where there is no air ventilation system except open windows and a fan, such as many urban apartments, the green application from the *Famulari Theory* stands alone and creates a space which reduces the infectiousness of the airborne flu virus. In places where there are interior ventilation and filtration systems, the *Famulari Theory* enhances the existing system to help reduce the airborne flu virus.

THE PSYCHOLOGICAL BENEFITS OF USING LIVING GREEN PLANTS IN THE *FAMULARI THEORY*

There are multiple psychological benefits of being in a space which has living plants. In studies, green design with plants has been shown to improve people's mental and physical health.

Image 10.12

This office space design is shown with and without plants. The plants not only improve the air quality but also create a space which is more appealing to spend time in.

The ability to increase mental well-being through green office is one benefit to implementing green design. People experience stress reduction through visual and physical interaction with green designs. Gardening, interior or exterior, can help reduce stress. People can see time and change with colors, growth and flowering of plants. Sound features with water elements can create an enjoyable atmospheric sound.

Employee and student productivity are also increased with interior green designs. Improve sinus health with plant scents and fresh air, as well as improving one's mental health and physical health, therefore reducing sick days. For students specifically, studies have shown that viewing and exposure to greenery while studying or researching improves retention of knowledge.

People who are exposed to green planted designs and can see them in sight while recovering have been shown to have lower stress, lower blood pressure, improve the pace of healing, and reduce hospitalization time. The book Healing Gardens by Cooper Marcus & Barnes, discusses the design philosophy of healing gardens. One study of an outdoor space in hospitals showed that 95 percent of the people surveyed had positive mood changes after spending time outside. When participants were asked which specific elements changed

Image 10.13

A bedroom space with and without an interior landscape. The plants create a more relaxing space.

their moods, more than 66 percent said trees, flowers, colors, seasonal changes, and greenery made a positive impact. 50 percent of the participants also mentioned that senses such as sound, scent and touch also had an effect. This included elements such as fresh air, birds chirping, and the sound of water (such as fountains).

The benefits of green design are not only valuable for the patients, but also for the practitioners, administrators and all users of the site. Medical practitioners and administrators who care for the visitors are also in need of taking care of themselves. One cannot care best for another unless they take care of their own personal health, mentally and physically. Also, people who attend appointments with patients are likely to be stressed or in need of healing. All people can favor from more self-care and joy in their own lives. Green spaces help improve focus, clarity and healing.

Gardens at hospitals have been shown not only to have patients and their families and friends attending, but also doctors and administrators. Selecting plants which bloom through the full year allows cycles of colors, scents, views, and illustrate time, change and growth through the garden design. Everyone who experiences a successful year-round blooming site can benefit with healing properties of plants.

In designing with the settings of healthcare, the more greenery, the better. This is not only for the mental health improvement, but for air quality improvement. Though healthcare facilities typically have an engineered system for all air quality cleaning, using green design helps support the engineered system.

Plants, water features, textures, and tactile experiences soothe the spirit. The sounds and scents of plants, water, wind and chimes create a mood, cadence, a spirit of calm and peace.

(Famulari, 2020)

PUTTING THE PIECES TOGETHER – THE TOTALITY OF THE APPLICATION

The likely rates of effectiveness of the *Famulari Theory* are in part determined by each of the six pieces, as well as their combined effect. Some of the pieces have rates of effectiveness determined based on studies, while others are based on science and the conditions in which plants live and grow.

1- *Temperature minimum of 70°F*

The temperature at which huwomxns feel comfortable, while allowing plants to grow and create conditions to have open stomata, is 70°F. Colder temperatures are also not effective at reducing the flu virus, but rather are spaces where the flu virus is able to stay infectious for longer periods.

2- *Plants with multiple stomata on the leaf surfaces*

Plants with stomata on the leaves allow plants to transpire (produce humidity). Humidity helps to lower the infectiousness of the airborne flu virus.

3- *Plants with multiple clumps of dense leaves with a high transpiration rate*

Plants with a high density of leaves which have stomata and high transpiration rates help to add humidity to the air to lower the infectiousness of the airborne flu, as well as having a leaf surface for the virus to stay on. The more leaf surfaces, the more space there is for the airborne flu virus to accumulate. The leaf surface with stomata produces a moist area in the millimeters next to the leaf. This moist area can reduce the infectiousness of the virus.

4- *Plants with rough leaf surfaces or with trichomes (plant hairs) on the leaf*

Plants with trichomes (plant hairs) have a rough surface – a surface where the virus can accumulate or stay on the leaf with plant hairs. Combine the densely growing plant, with high transpiration and a moist surface, as well as plant hairs on the leaves, and an ideal condition is created for the airborne virus to have reduced infectiousness.

5- *Relative humidity minimum of 43% or higher*

Relative humidity in the range of 43% or greater reduces the infectiousness of the flu virus to *less than* 14.6–22.2%. With a lower relative humidity, the effectiveness of reducing the infectiousness decreases. Creating an RH greater than 43% is five times more effective at reducing the flu viability than an RH of 7–23%. Adding humidity may require water features and humidifiers as well as plants.

6- *Air circulation to direct air with the airborne flu virus to the planted areas*

Studies for air circulation are specific to the site and type of air circulation and therefore have a great range of effectiveness. In this applied greening theory, air circulation is used to move the virus which is circulating in the air to the surface of the leaves where it can be accumulated. The virus can accumulate on the leaf while the infectiousness of it is reduced through humidity, temperature, and time.

It is the combination of the six pieces of the *Famulari Theory* which work together for the most effective solution. Though some pieces can stand alone to help reduce the infectiousness of the airborne virus, in combination, more conditions and surfaces applied together support and

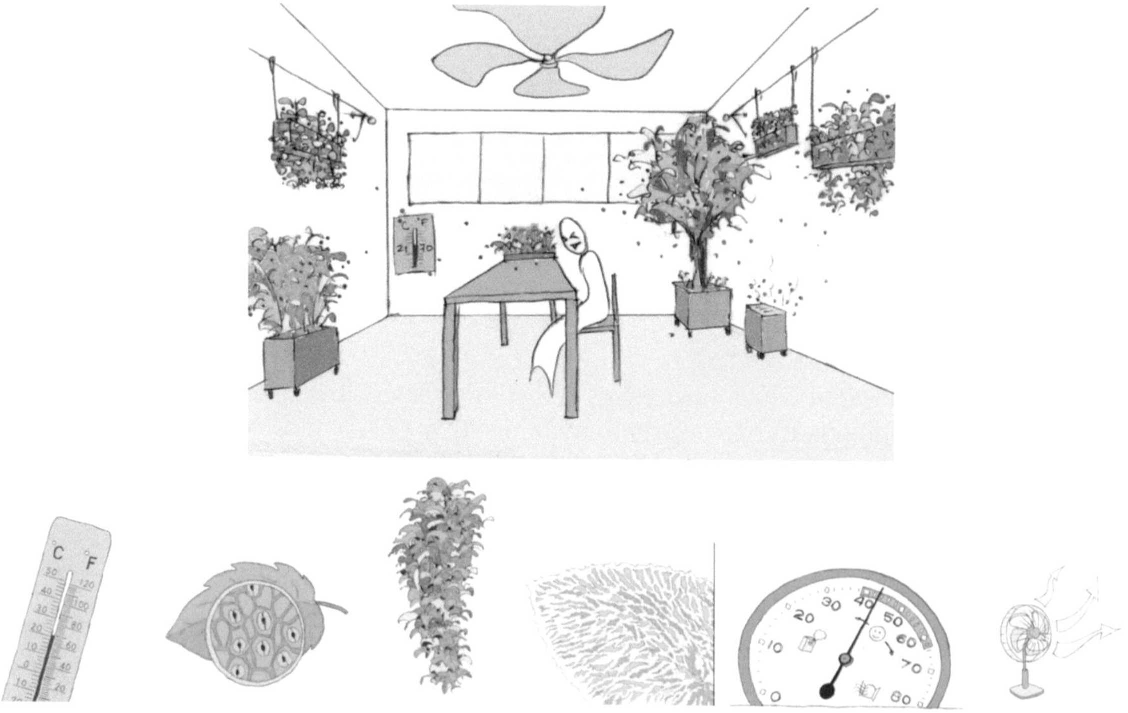

Image 10.14

The *Famulari Theory* is illustrated with the six pieces which reduce the infectiousness of the airborne flu. These include: (1) the temperature of the space as a minimum of 70°F; (2) using plants which have stomata on the leaves to help with transpiration (humidity); (3) using plants which have leaves which grow densely; (4) using plants with trichomes (plant hairs) on the leaves; (5) minimum of 43% humidity in the space; and (6) air circulation to move the air with viruses to the plant leaves and humidity.

Image 10.15

Living room with the *Famulari Theory* applied. A house with a family and guests is one of many settings where it is beneficial to have a healthy environment.

improve the effectiveness of reducing infectiousness. Additionally, with the effects of plants to lower stress, improve mental well-being, create joyful feelings, improve memory, and improve the environment – the full set of six pieces becomes even more effective for site design.

THINKING FORWARD

Creating spaces both large and small, both indoors and outdoors, for huwomxns to engage with plants is a healthy and joyful approach to living. Plants not only enrich the soul with their colors, textures, flowers, stunning shades of greens, and their daily changes, they also improve our physical health in ways which continue to be studied by people in diverse fields of arts and sciences. Working with the fields of art, design, science, and technology there are a multitude of ways in which we can engage greening design and plants for countless applications.

I encourage you to use not only this green theory in your spaces but to find new creative ways of combining knowledge and research to expand the greening field even further. This field is growing and has opportunities for applications in such unique ways. The *Famulari Theory* can be applied in more ways which this book illustrates. *Designing Green Spaces for Health* can be expanded to your site, no matter what your site is. Be open, be creative, and be green forward.

REFERENCES

AirFuji. (n.d.). Air HEPA vs MERV: The furnace filter battle. *AirFuji.* https://airfuji.com/hepa-vs-merv/ (retrieved 4 September 2020).

Eldman, L., & Clark, K. (2009, 18 March). Air filtration: Air filter media - An industry evolves. *Filtration Separation.* https://www.filtsep.com/filter%20media/features/air-filtration-air-filter-media-an-industry/ (retrieved 4 September 2020).

EPA. (n.d.). Indoor air quality (IAQ). Indoor air facts no. 4 (revised) sick building syndrome. Environmental Protection Agency. http://www.epa.gov/iaq/pubs/sbs.html (retrieved 4 September 2020).

Famulari, S. (2020). *Green Up! Sustainable Design Solutions for Healthier Work and Living Environments.* New York: Productivity Press. doi:10.4324/9780429297434

Joshi, S. M. (2008). The sick building syndrome. *Indian Journal of Occupational and Environmental Medicine, 12*(2), 61–64. doi:10.4103/0019-5278.43262.

NSC. (n.d.). IAQ fact sheet sick building syndrome, Environmental Health Center. National Safety Council. http://www.nsc.org/ehc/indoor/sbs.htm-8k- (retrieved 4 September 2020).

Bibliography

AirFuji. (n.d.). HEPA vs MERV: The furnace filter battle. *AirFuji*. https://airfuji.com/hepa-vs-merv/ (retrieved 4 September 2020).

Arizona State University. (2019, July 17). Plant viruses may be reshaping our world. *ScienceDaily*. www.sciencedaily.com/releases/2019/07/190717142645 (retrieved 1 June 2020).

Atrium Plants. (n.d.). How to beat flu this winter with houseplants. *Atrium Plants*. https://atriumplants.co.za/blogs/the-dirt/how-to-beat-flu-this-winter-with-houseplants (retrieved 7 June 2020).

Bailes, A. (2010, 7 June). The 4 factors of comfort. *Energy Vanguard*. https://www.energyvanguard.com/blog/24336/The-4-Factors-of-Comfort (retrieved 22 August 2020).

Bailey, R. (2019, August 15). What is the function of plant stomata? *Thoughts Co*. https://www.thoughtco.com/plant-stomata-function-4126012 (retrieved 2 August 2020).

Balique, F., Lecoq, H., Raoult, D., & Colson, P. (2015). Can plant viruses cross the kingdom border and be pathogenic to humans? *Viruses*, *7*(4), 2074–2098. doi:10.3390/v7042074

Bamogo, P. K. A., Brugidou, C., Sérémé, D., Tiendrébéogo, F., Djigma, F. W., Simpore, J., Lacombe, S., et al. (2019). Virus-based pharmaceutical production in plants: An opportunity to reduce health problems in Africa. *Virology Journal*, *16*, 167. doi:10.1186/s12985-019-1263-0

Beans, C. (2017). Phytoremediation advances in the lab but lags in the field. *Proceedings of the National Academy of Sciences of the United States of America (PNAS). 114*, 29. doi:10.1073/pnas.1707883114

Belis, C. A., Posini, E., Thunis, P.. (2013). Source apportionment of air pollution in the Danube region. http://iet.jrc.ec.europa.eu (retrieved 4 June 2020).

Bioadvanced. (n.d.). 5 benefits of houseplants. *BioAdvanced*. https://www.bioadvanced.com/articles/5-benefits-houseplants (retrieved 4 June 2020).

Brawner, M. (n.d.). Transpiration and why it matters. *Harlequin's Gardens*. https://harlequinsgardens.com/transpiration-and-why-it-matters/ (retrieved 4 June 2020).

Breyer, M. (2015). 5 health benefits of houseplants. *Treehugger*. https://www.treehugger.com/health/5-health-benefits-houseplants.html (retrieved 4 June 2020).

Britannica Online Encyclopedia. (n.d.). Succulent. *Britannica*. https://www.britannica.com/plant/succulent (retrieved 7 June 2020).

Carminati, A., Passioura, J. B., Zarebanadkouki, M., Ahmed, M. A., Ryan, P. R., Watt, M., & Delhaize, E. (2017). Root hairs enable high transpiration rates in drying soils. *New Phytologist*, *216*(3), 771–781. doi:10.1111/nph.14715

CBC Radio. (2019). A genetically modified houseplant could suck up dangerous indoor pollution. Canadian Broadcasting Corporation (CDC). https://www.cbc.ca/radio/quirks/jan-12-2019-medieval-woman-painters-houseplants-eat-pollution-viruses-that-kill-superbugs-and-more-1.4972835/a-genetically-modified-houseplant-could-suck-up-dangerous-indoor-air-pollution-1.4972842 (retrieved 1 June 2020).

CK-12. (n.d.). 11.22 virus structure-advanced. *CK-12*. https://www.ck12.org/book/ck-12-biology-advanced-concepts/section/11.22/ (retrieved 18 July 2020).

Eldman, L., & Clark, K. (2009, 18 March). Air filtration: Air filter media - An industry evolves. *Filtration Separation*. https://www.filtsep.com/filter%20media/features/air-filtration-air-filter-media-an-industry/ (retrieved 4 September 2020).

Elmore, W. (2017). Can my plants catch the flu? Plant viruses and transmission to hosts. University of Florida, Institute of Food and Agricultural Sciences (UF/IFAS). http://blogs.ifas.ufl.edu/pascoco/2017/12/29/can-plants-catch-flu-plant-viruses-transmission-hosts/ (retrieved 1 June 2020).

Emelda, M. (2017, 29 August). Difference between humidity and relative humidity. *Difference Between*. http://www.differencebetween.net/science/nature/difference-between-humidity-and-relative-humidity/ (retrieved 20 August 2020).

Environmental Filter. (2020, 16 March). Micro size of viruses. *Environmental Filter*. https://efiblog.wixsite.com/environmentalfilter/post/microns-of-viruses (retrieved 16 August 2020).

EPA. (2019, 3 April). What is a HEPA filter? Environmental Protection Agency. https://www.epa.gov/indoor-air-quality-iaq/what-hepa-filter-1 (retrieved 23 July 2020).

EPA. (n.d.). Indoor air quality (IAQ). Indoor air facts no. 4 (revised) sick building syndrome. Environmental Protection Agency. http://www.epa.gov/iaq/pubs/sbs.html (retrieved 4 September 2020).

Eva-Dry. (2020, 9 June). The difference between absolute, relative and specific humidity. *Eva-Dry*. https://www.eva-dry.com/humidity-difference-absolute-relative-specific/?doing_wp_cron=1598136187.8569369316101074218750 (retrieved 22 August 2020).

Famulari, S. (2020). *Green Up! Sustainable Design Solutions for Healthier Work and Living Environments*. New York: Productivity Press. doi:10.4324/9780429297434

Finnegan, M. J., Pickering, C. A., & Burge, P. S. (1984). The sick building syndrome: Prevalence studies. *BMJ, 289*, 1573–1575.

FluCamp. (n.d.). Do cold and flu viruses stay contagious out of the body? *FluCamp*. https://flucamp.com/do-cold-and-flu-viruses-stay-contagious-outside-of-the-body/ (retrieved 18 July 2020).

Foster, H. (2016). The reason for the season: Why flu strikes in winter. Harvard University, The Graduate School of Arts and Sciences, SITN, science in the news. http://sitn.hms.harvard.edu/flash/2014/the-reason-for-the-season-why-flu-strikes-in-winter/ (retrieved 18 July 2020).

Fox, S. (2010). Evidence of first virus that infects both plants and humans. *Popular Science*. https://www.popsci.com/science/article/2010-04/scientists-discover-first-virus-make-jump-plants-humans/ (retrieved 1 June 2020).

Fricke, W. (2019). Night-time transpiration- favouring growth? *Trends in Plant Science, 24*(4), 311–317. doi:10.1016/j.tplants.2019.01.007

Goldowitz Jimenez, I. (2018). What plants humidify the air: Learn about houseplants that increase humidity. *Gardening Know How*. https://www.gardeningknowhow.com/houseplants/hpgen/houseplants-that-increase-humidity.htm (retrieved 4 June 2020).

Greatorex, J. S., Page, R. F., Curran, M. D., Digard, P., Enstone, J. E., Wreghitt, T., Powell, P. P., Sexton, D. W., Vivancos, R., & Nguyen-Van-Tam, J. S. (2010). Effectiveness of common household cleaning agents in reducing the viability of human influenza A/H1N1. *PloS One*, *5*(2), e8987. doi:10.1371/journal.pone.0008987

Griffiths, H., & Males, J. (2017). Succulent plants. *Current Biology*, *27*(17), R890–R896. doi:10.1016/j.cub.2017.03.021

Hou, C. Y., & Schmitz, A. (2020, 21 January). This animation shows how far your sneeze can actually travel. *Business Insider*. https://www.businessinsider.com/how-far-sneeze-cough-germs-can-travel-2018-10 (retrieved 1 June 2020).

Jiwaji, M., Felicity Matcher, G., de Bruyn, M. M., Awino Awando, J., Moodley, H., Waterworth, D., & Jarvie, R.A., Dorrington, R. A. (2019). Providence virus: An animal virus that replicates in plants or a plant virus that infects and replicates in animal cells? *PloS One*. doi:10.1371/journal.pone.0217494

Joshi, S. M. (2008). The sick building syndrome. *Indian Journal of Occupational and Environmental Medicine*, *12*(2), 61–64. doi:10.4103/0019-5278.43262

Lange, N. R., & Schuster, D. P. (1999). The measurement of lung water. *Critical Care (London, England)*, *3*(2), R19–R24. doi:10.1186/cc342

Lawrence, L. (2017, 21 July). Why do water plants have stomata on upper part of their leaves? *Sciencing*. https://sciencing.com/why-do-water-plants-have-stomata-on-upper-part-of-their-leaves-13428558.html (retrieved 2 August 2020).

Lefeuvre, P., Martin, D. P., Elena, S. F., Shepherd, D. N., Roumagnac, P., & Varsani, A. (2019). Evolution and ecology of plant viruses. *Nature Reviews Microbiology, 17*, 632–644. doi:10.1038/s41579-019-0232-3

Live Science Staff. (2020). 11 (sometimes) deadly diseases that hopped across species. *Live Science*. https://www.livescience.com/12951-10-infectious-diseases-ebola-plague-influenza.html (retrieved 1 June 2020).

Mandal, B., & Jain, R. K. (2010). Can plant virus infect human being? *Indian Journal of Virology: An Official Organ of Indian Virological Society*, *21*(1), 92–93. doi:10.1007/s13337-010-0014-z

McGill, K. (2018). Seasonal flu virus: Why vaccines never go out of style. *Sci, The Dish on Science*. https://thedishonscience.stanford.edu/posts/seasonalfluvaccine/ (retrieved 18 July 2020).

Memarzadeh, F. (2013). Literature review: Room ventilation and airborne disease transmission. The American Society for Healthcare Engineering (ASHE) & The Facility Guidelines Institute. https://fgiguidelines.org/wp-content/uploads/2015/07/ASHE-FGI_Monograph_RoomVentilation.pdf (retrieved 4 December 2020).

National Weather Service. (n.d.). A discussion of water vapor, humidity, and dewpoint, and relationship of precipitation. National Weather Service. https://www.weather.gov/lmk/humidity (retrieved 22 August 2020).

Nielsen, P. V. (2009). Control of airborne infectious diseases in ventilated spaces. *Journal of the Royal Society, Interface*, *6*(Suppl 6), S747–S755. doi:10.1098/rsif.2009.0228.focus

Noti, J. D., Blachere, F. M., McMillen, C. M., Lindsley, W. G., Kashon, M. L., Slaughter, D. R., & Beezhold, D. H. (2013). High humidity leads to loss of infectious influenza virus from simulated coughs. *PloS One*, *8*(2): e57485. doi:10.1371/journal.pone.0057485

NSC. (n.d.). IAQ fact sheet sick building syndrome, Environmental Health Center. National Safety Council. http://www.nsc.org/ehc/indoor/sbs.htm-8k- (retrieved 4 September 2020).

Plant Air Purifier. (2016). U.S. Health Equipment Company, Inc. https://www.plantairpurifier.com/product_benefits_-_overview.html (retrieved 4 December 2020).

Plant and Soil Sciences elibrary. (2020). Transpiration - Factors affecting rates of transpiration. https://passel2.unl.edu/view/lesson/c242ac4fbaaf/6 (retrieved 4 June 2020).

Qian, H., & Zheng, X. (2018). Ventilation control for airborne transmission of human exhaled bio-aerosols in buildings. *Journal of Thoracic Disease*, *10*(Suppl 19), S2295–S2304. doi:10.21037/jtd.2018.01.24

Racaniello, V. (2009, 13 April). Viruses and the tree of life. *Small Things Considered*. https://schaechter.asmblog.org/schaechter/2009/04/viruses-and-the-tree-of-life.html (retrieved 4 December 2020).

Raffaele. (2020, 6 January). Houseplants that humidify the air: 50 plants evaluated. *Ohio Tropics*. https://www.ohiotropics.com/2020/01/06/houseplants-that-humidify-the-air-50-plants-evaluated/ (retrieved 4 June 2020).

Rawat, A. (2019, 11 November). Do you know which plants release oxygen at night? https://www.fnp.com/article/do-you-know-which-plants-release-oxygen-at-night (retrieved 22 August 2020).

Reviewon. (n.d.). The 5 different types of germs and their symptoms. *Reviewon*. https://reviewon.com/the-5-different-types-of-germs-and-their-characteristics.html#:~:text=%20The%205%20Different%20Types%20Of%20Germs%20,are%20single%20celled%20organisms%20which%20react...%20More%20 (retrieved 15 August 2020).

Robson, D. (2015). The real reasons germs spread in the winter. *BBC Future, Health*. https://www.bbc.com/future/article/20151016-the-real-reason-germs-spread-in-the-winter (retrieved 18 July 2020).

San Diego Zoo. (n.d.). Cactuses and succulents. San Diego Zoo. https://animals.sandiegozoo.org/plants/cactuses-succulents (retrieved 22 August 2020).

SAPS. (n.d.). Measuring stomatal density. Science & Plants for Schools. https://www.saps.org.uk/secondary/teaching-resources/299-measuring-stomatal-density (retrieved 20 August 2020).

Sheikh, M. A. (2018). Plant defense and counter defense by viruses. *Advances in Plant Pathology*, Josphert Ngui Kimatu, *IntechOpen*, doi:10.5772/intechopen.79114. https://www.intechopen.com/books/advances-in-plant-pathology/plant-defense-and-counter-defense-by-viruses (retrieved 18 July 2020).

Socrates Bardi, J. (2009, 14 June). The gross science of a cough and a sneeze. *Live Science*. https://www.livescience.com/3686-gross-science-cough-sneeze.html (retrieved 1 June 2020).

Stierwalt, S. (2020, 13 April). What's the difference between germs, bacteria, and viruses? *Quick and Dirty*. https://www.quickanddirtytips.com/education/science/whats-the-difference-between-germs-bacteria-and-viruses (retrieved 15 August 2020).

Succulent. (2018). Seven benefits of growing succulents in your home. Succulents. https://www.succulents.net/7-benefits-growing-succulents-home/ (retrieved 7 June 2020).

Succulent City. (2020). 5 succulents that are considered herbaceous. Succulent City. https://succulentcity.com/5-succulents-that-are-considered-herbaceous/ (retrieved 7 June 2020).

Tang, J. W. (2009). The effect of environmental parameters on the survival of airborne infectious agents. *Journal of the Royal Society, Interface*, *6*(Suppl 6), S737–S746. doi:10.1098/rsif.2009.0227.focus

Theory. (2020). In *Oxford Online Dictionary*. https://en.oxforddictionaries.com/definition/theory (retrieved 5 December 2020)

Tufekci, Z. (2020). We need to talk about ventilation. How is it that six months into a respiratory pandemic, we are still doing so little to mitigation airborne transmission? *The Atlantic*. https://www.theatlantic.com/health/archive/2020/07/why-arent-we-talking-more-about-airborne-transmission/614737/ (retrieved 4 December 2020).

United States Geological Survey (USGS). (n.d.). Evapotranspiration and the water cycle. https://www.usgs.gov/special-topic/water-science-school/science/evapotranspiration-and-water-cycle?qt-science_center_objects=0#qt-science_center_objects (retrieved 4 June 2020).

University of Florida. (n.d.). Trichomes. https://irrecenvhort.ifas.ufl.edu/plant-prop-glossary/01-biology/02-cell-types/11-celltypes-trichome.html (retrieved 5 December 2020).

Unusual Seeds. (2019). 5 ways succulents can help you stay healthy. *Unusual Seeds*. https://unusualseeds.net/5-ways-succulents-can-help-you-stay-healthy/ (retrieved 7 June 2020).

Valeiko, K. (2019). 5 benefits of having succulents in your home. *Red*. https://www.redonline.co.uk/interiors/homeware/a526209/five-health-benefits-of-having-succulents-in-your-home/ (retrieved 7 June 2020).

Westover, J. (n.d.). What can make a majesty palm turn brown at the tips? *Hunker.* https://www.hunker.com/12552844/what-can-make-a-majesty-palm-turn-brown-at-the-tips (retrieved 4 June 2020)

Williams, S., Boehm, M., & Qu, F. (2017). Viral diseases of plants. *Ohioline Ohio State Extension.* https://ohioline.osu.edu/factsheet/plpath-gen-5 (retrieved 1 June 2020).

Woodford, C. (2020, 27 June). HEPA filters. *Explain that Stuff.* https://www.explainthatstuff.com/hepafilters.html (retrieved 23 July 2020).

Yang, W., & Marr, L. C. (2011). Dynamics of airborne influenza. A virus indoors and dependence on humidity. *PloS One*, *6*(6): e21481.

Zach, O. (2018). Top 10 plants for a healthy indoor succulent garden. *Plant Catalyst.* http://www.plantcatalyst.com/2018/01/17/top-10-plants-for-a-healthy-indoor-succulent-garden/ (retrieved 7 June 2020).

Image Credits

FRONT COVER AND BACK COVER

Images – Stevie Famulari, Gds

INTRODUCTION

Images I.1, I.2 – Stevie Famulari, Gds

CHAPTER 1

Images icon, 1.1, 1.2, 1.3, 1.4, 1.5 – Stevie Famulari, Gds

CHAPTER 2

Images 2.1, 2.10, 2.11, 2.12, 2.13, 2.14 – Stevie Famulari, Gds
Images 2.2, 2.3, 2.4, 2.5, 2.6, 2.7, 2.8, 2.9 – Trenton Moore
Image 2.15 – Anna Aybetova/Shutterstock
Image 2.16 – Kathryn Roach/Shutterstock
Image 2.17 – Kusalodom/Shutterstock
Image 2.18 – lorenza62/Shutterstock
Image 2.19 – COULANGES/Shutterstock
Image 2.20 – Agata Buczek/Shutterstock
Image 2.21 – Charlotte Bleijenberg/Shutterstock
Image 2.22 – Ninja Artist/Shutterstock
Image 2.23 – FreshPaint/Shutterstock
Image 2.24 – pixmeeup/Shutterstock
Image 2.25 – lito_lakwatsero/Shutterstock

CHAPTER 3

Images 3.1, 3.9, 3.10, 3.11, 3.12, 3.13, 3.14, 3.22 – Stevie Famulari, Gds
Images 3.2, 3.3, 3.4, 3.5, 3.6, 3.7, 3.8 – Trenton Moore
Image 3.15 – WR7/Shutterstock

Image 3.16 – aniana/Shutterstock
Image 3.17 – Francisco Herrera/Shutterstock
Image 3.18 – rivermartin/Shutterstock
Image 3.19 – Martin Fowler/Shutterstock
Image 3.20 – riphoto3/Shutterstock
Image 3.21 – dugwy39/Shutterstock
Image 3.23 – Prostock-studio/Shutterstock
Image 3.24 – Mrs_ya/Shutterstock

CHAPTER 4

Images 4.1, 4.8, 4.9, 4.10, 4.11, 4.12, 4.13 – Stevie Famulari, Gds
Images 4.2 – Edvard Nalbantjan/Shutterstock
Image 4.3 – ArtEvent ET/Shutterstock
Image 4.4 – Kit Leong/Shutterstock
Image 4.5 – Stanislav71/Shutterstock
Image 4.6 – bezikus/Shutterstock
Image 4.7 – D. Ribeiro/Shutterstock
Image 4.14 – Lienda Yunita Apponno/Shutterstock
Image 4.15 – shutting/Shutterstock
Image 4.16 – Andrejs Marcenko/Shutterstock
Image 4.17 – FLORESPHOTOGRAPHIC/Shutterstock
Image 4.18 – Vitaly Raduntsev/Shutterstock
Image 4.19 – Yundengogo/Shutterstock
Image 4.20 – Julian Popov/Shutterstock
Image 4.21 – Esstock/Shutterstock
Image 4.22 – Kat KTM/Shutterstock
Image 4.23 – Matej Kastelic/Shutterstock

CHAPTER 5

Images 5.1, 5.9, 5.10, 5.11, 5.12, 5.13, 5.14, 5.15, 5.20, 5.22, 5.30 – Stevie Famulari, Gds
Images 5.2, 5.3, 5.4, 5.5, 5.6, 5.7, 5.8 – Trenton Moore
Image 5.15 - Pixel-Shot/Shutterstock
Image 5.16 - Maritxu/Shutterstock
Image 5.17 - Hanjo Hellmann/Shutterstock
Image 5.18 - Esteban Martinena Guerrer/Shutterstock
Image 5.19 - nook kie/Shutterstock
Image 5.21 - VarnakovR/Shutterstock
Image 5.23 - COULANGES/Shutterstock
Image 5.24 - Teerasak Chinnasot/Shutterstock
Image 5.25 - allgoo/Shutterstock
Image 5.26 - Sample Stars/Shutterstock
Image 5.27 - Fluff Media/Shutterstock
Image 5.28 - Artit Wongpradu/Shutterstock
Image 5.29 - MBLifestyle/Shutterstock

CHAPTER 6

Images 6.1, 6.8, 6.9, 6.10, 6.11 – Stevie Famulari, Gds
Images 6.2, 6.3, 6.4, 6.5, 6.6, 6.7 – Trenton Moore
Image 6.12 – Federico Rostagno/Shutterstock
Image 6.13 – atiger/Shutterstock
Image 6.14 – Jana Kollarova/Shutterstock
Image 6.15 – Lui12/Shutterstock
Image 6.16 – Halit Omer/Shutterstock
Image 6.17 – Daria Chernykh/Shutterstock
Image 6.18 – Cr3ativ3 Pixel/Shutterstock
Image 6.19 – Iva Villi/Shutterstock
Image 6.20 – LeWid/Shutterstock
Image 6.21 – yyma/Shutterstock
Image 6.22 – Dmytro Surkov/Shutterstock

CHAPTER 7

Images 7.1, 7.7, 7.8, 7.9, 7.10 – Stevie Famulari, Gds
Images 7.2, 7.3, 7.4, 7.5, 7.6 – Trenton Moore
Image 7.11a – Koxae Sun/Shutterstock
Image 7.11b – RPPD/Shutterstock
Image 7.11c – Cuchawan/Shutterstock
Image 7.11d – Eloy_CM/Shutterstock
Image 7.12 – Przemyslaw Muszynski/Shutterstock
Image 7.13 – Asian Images/Shutterstock
Image 7.14 – Pefkos/Shutterstock
Image 7.15 – Peter Turner Photography/Shutterstock
Image 7.16 – JL Jahn/Shutterstock
Image 7.17 – Denisky19/Shutterstock
Image 7.18 – RukiMedia/Shutterstock
Image 7.19 – Foto by M/Shutterstock
Image 7.20 – Aliaksandr Bukatsich/Shutterstock

CHAPTER 8

Images icon, 8.1 – Stevie Famulari, Gds
Image 8.2, 8.8, 8.9, 8.10, 8.11, 8.12, 8.14 – Stevie Famulari, Gds
Image 8.3 – VectorMine/Shutterstock
Image 8.4 – Alila Medical Media/Shutterstock
Image 8.5 – Designua/Shutterstock
Image 8.6 – Zvitaliy/Shutterstock
Image 8.7 – Elena Kazanskaya/Shutterstock
Image 8.13a – Jomic/Shutterstock
Image 8.13b – Monkey Business Images/Shutterstock
Image 8.13c – DifferR/Shutterstock

Image 8.13d – PhotoNastya91/Shutterstock
Image 8.13e – Gaf_Lila/Shutterstock
Image 8.13f – porjai kittawornrat/Shutterstock

CHAPTER 9

Images icon, 9.1, 9.24 – Stevie Famulari, Gds
Image 9.2 – Ardely/Shuttertock
Image 9.3 – BlueRingMedia/Shutterstock
Image 9.4 – Victoria Tucholka/Shutterstock
Image 9.5 – Imageman/Shutterstock
Image 9.6 – Gleti/Shutterstock
Image 9.7 – Cornel Constantin/Shutterstock
Image 9.8 – Kicky_Princess/Shutterstock
Image 9.9 – JoeFotoSS/Shutterstock
Image 9.10 – dropStock/Shutterstock
Image 9.11 – armifello/Shutterstock
Image 9.12 – Adisa/Shutterstock
Image 9.13 – Coplay/Shutterstock
Image 9.14 – SunilDX/Shutterstock
Image 9.15 – Jakinnboaz/Shutterstock
Images 9.16, 9.17 – BlueRingMedia/Shutterstock
Image 9.18 – Lamyai/Shutterstock
Image 9.19 – Pam Walker/Shutterstock
Image 9.20 – A Hicks/Shutterstock
Image 9.21 – Maritxu/Shutterstock
Image 9.22 – New Africa/Shutterstock
Image 9.23 – Note On The Earth/Shutterstock
Image 9.25 – olrat/Shutterstock

CHAPTER 10

Image icon, 10.1, 10.3, 10.4, 10.6, 10.12a, 10.13b, 10.14, 10.15 – Stevie Famulari, Gds
Image 10.2 – P. OCHASANOND/Shutterstock
Image 10.5 – 1989studio/Shutterstock
Image 10.7 – CapturePB/Shutterstock
Image 10.8 – DENYSOFF/Shutterstock
Image 10.9 – RF-2020/Shutterstock
Image 10.10 – Sucharas Wongpeth/Shutterstock
Image 10.11 – Oleg L/Shutterstock
Image 10.12b, 10.13b – Trenton Moore

Index